The *Pulpit Ministry* of the *Pastors*
of River Road Church, Baptist
Richmond, Virginia

Edited by

William Powell Tuck

The publication of this book is sponsored by the Endowment Fund of River Road Church, Baptist, Richmond, Virginia.

Photography by Warren F. Johnson

Sermon by James Slatton, "The Gift," from *Proclaiming the Baptist Vision: The Priesthood of All Believers*, ed. Walter B. Shurden (Macon, GA: Smyth & Helwys, 1993), is used by permission.

© 2012 River Road Church, Baptist

Richmond, Virginia 23229

Published in the United States by Nurturing Faith Inc., Macon GA,

www.nurturingfaith.net.

Library of Congress Cataloging-in-Publication Data is available.

ISBN 978-1-938514-10-4

All rights reserved. Printed in the United States of America.

To the congregation of River Road Church, Baptist,
which has always given its pastors a free and open pulpit and
which has expected its pastors to share their best preaching gifts in the
proclamation of the Good News

Other Books by William Powell Tuck

The Way for All Seasons
Facing Grief and Death
The Struggle for Meaning (editor)
Knowing God: Religious Knowledge in the Theology of John Baillie
Our Baptist Tradition
Ministry: An Ecumenical Challenge (editor)
Getting Past the Pain
A Glorious Vision
The Bible as Our Guide for Spiritual Growth (editor)
Authentic Evangelism: Sharing the Good News with Sense and Sensitivity
The Lord's Prayer Today
Christmas Is for the Young . . . Whatever Their Age
Through the Eyes of a Child
Love as a Way of Living
The Compelling Faces of Jesus
The Left Behind Fantasy: The Theology Behind the Left Behind Tales
The Ten Commandments: Their Meaning Today
Facing Life's Ups and Downs
The Church in Today's World
The Church Under the Cross
Modern Shapers of Baptist Thought in America
The Journey to the Undiscovered Country: What's Beyond Death?
A Pastor Preaching: Toward a Theology of the Proclaimed Word

Contents

Foreword vii
Preface ix

David Earl Browning (Pastor, 1947-1950) 1
    The Mysteries of Life 3
    A Religion Worse Than None 9
    The Voice of Little Men 15
    The Master Speaks 21
    Christianity Confronts Communism 25
    This Is My Body 31

Woodrow Wilson Hasty (Pastor, 1950-1964) 33
    A Dangerous Book 35
    On Being a Christian 41
    Life's Greatest Lesson 47
    Facing the Days Ahead as a Christian 55
    To Which Church Would Jesus Belong? 63
    What Should You Tell a Child about God? 69

Vernon Britt Richardson (Pastor, 1964-1970) 77
    My Dream for This Church 81
    Meaning in Material 87
    The Story in Our Stained Glass Window 93
    A Church You Can Believe In 99
    The Environmental Crisis 103
    Live on Leftovers 109

James Hoyt Slatton (Pastor, 1971-2003) 113
    The Word, Divine and Human.. 117
    For Such a Time as This... 125
    Jacob: God's Unlikely Choice... 133
    The Gift 139
    The Resurrection—After Easter.. 145
    Overtaken by Easter... 153

Michael James Clingenpeel (Pastor, 2004-present) 163
    The Act of Surrender 167
    The Next Chapter in the Story 173
    Living with the End in Sight.. 181
    The Glorious Gift of Music 187
    The Color of Water 193
    A Speechless God and a Lonely Listener 199

Foreword

Easter is experienced every Sunday at River Road Church, Baptist, in Richmond, Virginia. It is evident in the congregation that assembles in high expectation of worship. It exudes in the grand music of the Christian faith presented through voice and instruments, as well as the king of instruments. It also appears from the pulpit where the resurrection message is repeated through a variety of themes and subjects. Easter may be a once-a-year holy day for most Christian churches, but at River Road it is a continuum.

The preached Word has been central among the River Road experiences through five pastorates spanning sixty-five years. It has been characterized as a search for truth. Vernon Richardson, a pastor who left a lasting imprint upon the church, put it this way:

> [River Road is] a church where we will be able to believe our beliefs. They ought to be true to the message of Scripture, for ours is an historical religion, intellectually respectable, responsibly held, subject to review in the light of new knowledge, and a witness to the whole of Christ's church, not to an isolated fragment of it.

James Slatton, the pastor with the longest occupancy of the pulpit, once said: "We must all find the truth for ourselves. Truth is never wrapped in cellophane and handed out predigested. Well, it often is, actually, but you should not swallow it whole that way." Truth is respected and examined from the River Road pulpit.

In the course of nearly seven decades, the pastors who occupied the pulpit have addressed many issues. David Browning, the founding pastor, considered communism. As early as 1970, Vernon Richardson preached about environmental issues. Nine years later, James Slatton delivered a sermon on the central issues that divided the Southern Baptist Convention and became known in short as "the controversy." He also prepared a new sermon in the few days between September 11, 2001, and the next Sunday. "We mourn not only the dead," said the pastor. "We mourn also the loss of something more. What seems lost, and what we have begun to mourn, is a sense of freedom and security in which we moved about just a few short days ago."

From the crow's nest pulpit in the church's sanctuary, the pastor may appear calm, cool, and collected. No one is aware of the nerves beneath the skin. Finally, in a sermon delivered as pastor emeritus, Jim Slatton confessed: "I never came or come into the pulpit without my heart being up in my throat. If I look under control, it's sheer theater."

In this collection of a few choice sermons among the many delivered at River Road, we must imagine what those in the pews never realized—the energy and emotion that privately were poured into the creation of the sermons, the hopes and aspirations of the preacher, the long unseen years of preparation that gave foundation to a twenty-minute message. And the reader can find the Easter message—one small nuance of it—carefully crafted within each sermon.

Fred Anderson

(Fred Anderson, a member of River Road Church, is executive director of the Virginia Baptist Historical Society and the Center for Baptist Heritage and Studies located on the campus of the University of Richmond.)

Preface

Preaching has always had a central place at River Road Church, Baptist. With an early connection to the University of Richmond faculty and students and the initial worship held in the university's Cannon Memorial Chapel, this congregation, from its inception, has expected well-crafted, thoughtful, challenging, and intellectually informed preaching. The pastors who filled the pulpit of this congregation since its beginning in 1945 have not disappointed the congregation. As John Killinger reminds us:

> Preaching, at its best, is not a solo task. It is done by an individual, but it is the sum of many things—of the community of faith, the Bible the community holds at its center, the tradition of proclamation it has nurtured, and the gifts, experiences, and artifices of the preacher.[1]

The congregation of River Road Church helped form and shape lofty expectations of the preaching event in its sacred worship space. In fact, the very structure where worship takes place for this congregation played a large role over the years in preaching expectations. Granted, the current worship structure was not always a part of the regular worship, but plans for such a structure were designed early in its infancy.

The formative worship in the chapel on the university campus, the design of the university chapel for worship with its divided chancel and lofty architecture, and the beautifully planned and anticipated sanctuary all shaped the expectations for elevated preaching from the pulpit. "The proclamation of the gospel," Jürgen Moltmann asserts, "always belongs within a community, for every language lives in a community or creates one."[2] The River Road Church community without question helped shape the dynamic preaching from the church's pulpit.

The layout of the sanctuary itself beckons the worshipper to high expectations. On entering the building, designed in a Colonial style of architecture, one's eyes are immediately drawn to the high ceiling that magnifies the sense of calling into the presence of holiness. Looking down the center aisle, eyes are drawn to the cross on the communion table and to the stained glass window depicting Jesus as preacher, teacher, and healer. An open Bible is on the communion table reminding us of the story of redemption and God's abiding love for humanity. From the church lectern, the Scriptures are read each week. The church building itself is shaped like a cross, reminding the worshipper of the one who laid down his life on a cross.

The pulpit in the sanctuary is elevated up high, not to glorify the preacher, but so the preacher can be seen and heard more easily. The pulpit rests on a chalice-shaped pedestal in the nave of the church and is set out among the congregation to attest to the reality that the pastor is a part of that community of faith.

Thomas Long, the distinguished professor of preaching at Emory University in Atlanta, Georgia, states that the preacher must be seen from two perspectives. "First, in every way the preacher is a part of the congregation, a member of the assembly who rises from the midst of the gathered people to perform the task of preaching." But Long continues to note that the preacher also secondly "moves to a new position, getting up from the congregation to stand in front of the community."[3] The preacher has been called by the congregation for the very function of being a proclaimer, but he continues to be a part of the worshipping community.

The pulpit in the River Road Church has six sides, which depict that the one speaking here is not perfect, but, like all persons, is imperfect and incomplete as he or she proclaims the message as he or she understands it. We remember the number seven was the biblical number for perfection or completeness. While the preacher seeks to proclaim holy truth, the preacher is also a human with imperfections.

The image of "the shield of faith" is located around the top of the pulpit and depicts the preacher's dependence on faith as the Word is heralded. The canopy over the pulpit dates to the ancient past when nothing in worship was to be uncovered, including the heads of those who worshipped in the building. Today, it serves as a sounding board to assist in the hearing of the preached Word. The "wine glass-shape" of the pulpit pedestal reminds us that Jesus is the one who brings us "new wine," or new life, as we respond to the redeeming Word proclaimed from the pulpit. Vernon Richardson's sermon, "Meaning in Material," gives a vivid description of the church sanctuary, the pulpit, and the meaning of all its components.

The membership of River Road Church, Baptist, includes a wide spectrum of persons of varying educational attainments, wide economic levels, and all ages from children to seniors. They represent a variety of careers including merchants, trades, professions, community leaders, and educational faculty in the local schools, colleges, graduate schools, and seminaries. No matter the educational level of the membership, the church sought a highly educated clergy. The pastors called to serve River Road Church came with advanced graduate studies and earned doctor's degrees.

The five preachers in this volume span almost seven decades. Each stayed a length of time to accomplish the challenges he faced in the building up of the congregation and the enhancement of the spiritual life of the membership. The third pastor, Vernon Richardson, had his tenure cut short by illness and death. James Slatton was pastor for thirty-one years, almost half the life of the church. Each preacher brought different gifts of preaching, management styles, craftsmanship, and vision.

Most of the sermons in this collection were available in complete manuscript form, such as the ones delivered by Woodrow Hasty, Vernon Richardson, James Slatton, and Michael Clingenpeel. The sermons crafted by David Browning, now deceased, were only available in outline form except for two, "The Mysteries of Life" and "This Is My Body." The outlines, however, were thorough, and made it possible to flesh them out. The exact dates when some of Browning's sermons were preached at River Road could not be determined due to the lack of many church bulletins during that time period. All of the sermons were preached at River Road Church with the possible exception of the two manuscript sermons by Browning. They are included because they give a good example of Browning's preaching. Unfortunately, we had few of his sermons in our collection. I selected the sermons by Browning, Hasty, and Richardson but gave Slatton and Clingenpeel the opportunity to select their own sermons for inclusion in this collection.

This volume offers the reader a unique look into almost seventy years of preaching by the pastors of this special church. If the occasion of the sermon is known or the date it was delivered is known, then one or both is included in a note with the sermon. The sermons address a variety of needs and occasions. Some of them were preached many years ago, but still have a freshness and contemporary tone. These sermons can still inspire, challenge, direct, and encourage a quest for deeper awareness of Christ and the meaning of the Christian faith and how it relates to our lives today.

Fred Craddock, who taught both preaching and New Testament and lectured and preached around the country and the world, declared that preaching finds power in its appropriateness to the context in which it is preached. In other words, he said "preaching has to fit." "That's why the preacher *par excellence* in this country," he asserts, "is the pastor, because the pastor is able to say the word that fits."[4] In this collection of sermons from five different pastors who spoke in different decades, the sermons still speak today because they fit the occasion when they were preached. And they fit the needs of the congregation known as River Road Church, Baptist.

I want to express appreciation to Barbara Jackson for her assistance in locating sermons by the early pastors of River Road Church in the church archives and for her special editorial work. I also want to thank Sandi Bassett for her typing of many of the sermons in this collection, especially the ones by Browning that she typed from his outlines, scanning many others and assisting in various other ways. A special word of credit is also extended to Warren Johnson for the picture of the River Road Church pulpit on the cover of the book and photographs of the portraits of the former pastors and of Michael Clingenpeel, the current pastor. Special appreciation is extended to the Endowment Fund of River Road Church for underwriting the publication of this collection of sermons. My prayer is that this collection will continue to affirm the importance of the preaching ministry of River Road Church, Baptist, and encourage the congregation to maintain its strong support of this church.

William Powell Tuck

Notes

[1] John Killinger, *Fundamentals of Preaching*, 2nd ed. (Minneapolis: Fortress Press, 1996), 1.

[2] Jürgen Moltmann, *The Church in the Power of the Spirit* (New York: Harper & Row, 1977), 224.

[3] Thomas G. Long, *The Witness of Preaching*, 2nd ed. (Louisville: Westminster John Knox, 2005), 16.

[4] Fred B. Craddock, *Craddock on the Craft of Preaching*, ed. Lee Sparks and Kathryn Hayes Sparks (St. Louis: Chalice Press, 2011), 119.

David Earl Browning
(Pastor, 1947-1950)

David Earl Browning was born on March 13, 1913, in Texarkana, Texas, and attended Texarkana Junior College and graduated from Ouachita Baptist University with a B.A. degree. He received the Th.M. and Ph.D. degrees from the Southern Baptist Theological Seminary in Louisville, Kentucky.

He married LaMena N. Nichols on June 16, 1933, and they had four sons. The family grew to include ten grandchildren and sixteen great-grandchildren.

His first pastorate was at Friendship Baptist Church near Redwater, Texas. While in seminary, he served as pastor of Bethany Baptist Church in Louisville. Following his graduation from seminary, he became pastor of First Baptist Church in North Wilkesboro, North Carolina.

Dr. Edward Pruden, pastor of the First Baptist Church in Washington, D.C., recommended Dr. Browning to the search committee of the fledgling River Road Church, then meeting on the University of Richmond campus. He accepted the call of the church and became its first pastor. During his brief tenure, the church grew from seventy members to 172, and a master plan for the church was developed that is close to what the church buildings are like today. The plans and construction of the chapel building were begun under Browning and were occupied in September of 1950, but were not fully completed until September of 1951. In July of 1950, Browning accepted a call to become the pastor of First Baptist Church in Harrisburg, Pennsylvania.

Later, Dr. Browning would serve as pastor of First Baptist Church, Troy, Alabama; Valley Park Baptist Church, Montgomery, Alabama; First Baptist Church, Eufaula, Alabama; Laurel Forks Baptist Church, Boone, North Carolina; Genoa Baptist Church, Texarkana, Arkansas; and Summer Hill Road Baptist Church, Texarkana, Texas. He served as interim pastor and supply preacher in numerous other churches across the South.

In concert with his preaching ministry, he also taught for twenty-three years at Alabama State University and ten years at Appalachian State University. In service to the denomination, he was on the Stewardship Commission of the Southern Baptist Convention and the administrative committee of the Executive Board of the Alabama State Baptist Convention, and was chairman of the program committee of the Pennsylvania Baptist Convention and speaker at the Pennsylvania Baptist Convention Pastor's Conference.

Dr. Browning was noted for his love of painting and for writing poetry. Samples of his paintings and pictures of the quilts his wife created appear in the booklet titled *Colorful Companions*, edited by their son, Philip Browning. Samples of Browning's poems, including one of his last poems, "Uncreation," published in *Theology Today* in July of 2005, are found in *A Beautiful Journey*, edited by Philip Browning, and in *Auburn Reflections*.

Dr. Browning died on March 3, 2009, in Auburn, Alabama, just ten days short of his ninety-sixth birthday.

The Mysteries of Life
Psalm 46:10

It was Robert Browning, the poet, who said:

> Grow old along with me!
> The best is yet to be,
> The last of life, for which the first was made;
> Our times are in His hand
> Who saith "A whole I planned,
> Youth shows but half: trust God: see all, nor be afraid."[1]

And we have grown older! But it is the best time of life. At our age we have a vast storehouse of memories; the memories of youth are limited.

In having grown old we are keenly aware of the mysteries of life. Do you remember the song of years ago when Jeanette MacDonald and Nelson Eddy sang: "Ah! Sweet mystery of life, at last I've found thee"? I do not know what they found other than life is a mystery—all life.

In our time together I want to remind you again of the past, the present, and the future of mysteries with which you have been confronted. And I do so for these reasons:

- To stimulate your thinking.
- In conversations with each other it is a good experience.
- To remember that which we have confronted in life, therein lies the God of grace and glory—who knows it all. Our trust in this fact will keep us steady and assured that life is worth living, and the best possible of all lives.

I believe there is a need for this exercise. We are living in times that become fast and faster. In this rapidly growing pace we have witnessed the flaunting of sacred values, and too often we are unmindful that . . .

This is the age of the half-read page,
The quick cash and the most cash,
The bright nights with the nerves tight,
The plane-hop and the brief stop;
The lamp-tan in a short span,
The big shot in a good spot,
The brain-strain and the heart pain:
And the fun is gone![2]

There is a voice of wisdom, out of the ancient past, for us: "Be still and know that I am God," the God of all life, all knowledge, of all grace and glory.

Life itself is a mystery. What is it that gives the "throb" to all living things? The living animals, trees, flowers, butterflies, gnats, and man—the apex of all creation—find life by God.

The life of the human body is a mystery: Look at how marvelously it is put together and functions. I've not made a decision for my blood to start flowing or my heart to keep beating. Aren't you glad that you cannot hear the blood flowing through your veins? And if the decibel count were raised in all the functions of the body, how much could we stand?

There are daily mysteries—some that get on our nerves. As someone gave an account: The traffic lane you changed, thinking it would be faster, only to find out it was slower than the one you left.

And there is the mystery of "traveling honey." You are sitting at a table removed from me by several tables, and I am not eating honey; but very soon I feel it on the handle of my knife.

These mysteries from ancient life: the pyramids, the Sphinx, and the disappearance of civilizations—like that of the Aztec . . .

Have you thought about the miracles in nature lately? There is the power of gravity. The child wins his first battle in life when he takes the first step—gravity is coped with! Think of the migration of birds. There is the Arctic tern that migrates 7,000 miles to its birthplace. There are millions of butterflies that migrate from and to the United States. And whales and fish migrate to their place of birth. Have you read of a certain species of spider that wears a web in the form of a sail, and catches the wind and is borne from this continent to Europe?

> Shadows are a mystery.
> You cannot measure their thickness,
> Nor do they have weight.
> You cannot scoop them up and shelve them,
> Nor fold them, nor stock them.
> There are things that do not cast a shadow:
> The beauty of a rose,
> The aroma of perfume,
> The revolutionary idea,
> The bubbling of a stream,
> The tide of an ocean.
>
> There are things which cast shadows. Even God!
> One Saint affirmed his abiding
> Under the shadow of the almighty.
> And when we bask in His Shadow,
> And go out into the world,
> We cast the shadow of Christ
> In which others can be healed and
> Find the joy of life.[3]

Have you wondered about time? Every living person has one thing he possesses and that is "owned" by every living person: time. All we have is the present, for the past has gone and the future lies ahead. Further, you cannot create more time for yourself or for others.

And there is the mystery of the mind. The brain is the vehicle of the mind. It is a mystery how the brain, made up of chemistry and electricity, can produce a thought. And think of the storehouse of memories! The brain has the ability to recall; we call it memory. And the proof that we do have memory is the fact that we forget!

And there is the power of intuition. Immanuel Kant, the German ethicist, tells us of a time when he and a friend were in conversation. Kant broke off the conversation and said, "My friend's house in on fire!" His friend lived two miles away. This was a time before telephones, radio, telegraphs, and fast transportation. Later, Kant received a letter from his friend stating that his house was lost in fire at a specific time and day. Kant recalled that it was the same time he broke the conversation with his friend.

In our Christian faith, Paul reminds us of these mysteries: the church, marriage, lawlessness, godliness, and the gospel. The power of prayer or intercessory prayer is attested to throughout the Bible.

In our times we are aware of those who are recipients of unjust triumph. We wonder about those who make fortune off of drugs, pornography, and "white slavery." And we are baffled by the "good citizens" who loot pension funds.

Let us bring this whole matter down on our personal level. There are questions. We ask: "What am I?" A person of stimulus and response only, or we are only "what we eat"? We are of the soil, ground, but more than that. We are created in the image of God, having the power to think and freedom to dream. We are "living souls." And "God breathed on man and he became a living soul."

And there is the question, "Why am I?" Why was I born in 1913, in Waco, Texas, the United States of America, rather than in China in the second century B.C.? Why am I who I am?

And then there is the third question, "Who am I?" That is to say, first, in whose life have I played such a part that if tomorrow I die, who would miss me? My wife, my sons, my kinsmen, and some friends. And the circle fades. No one in China would miss me. No Eskimo would miss me.

And who am I? That is, in the second place, to whom do we belong? We did not create ourselves; therefore we do not own ourselves. We belong to God. Wordsworth knew when he wrote:

> Our birth is but a sleep and a forgetting:
> The soul that rises with us, our life's Star,
> Hath had elsewhere its setting,
> And cometh from afar:
> Not in entire forgetfulness,
> And not in utter nakedness,
> But trailing clouds of glory do we come
> From God, who is our home.[4]

In conclusion, I do not know how you have confronted these mysteries, especially those of suffering, pain, loneliness, and broken dreams. I do remind you there is one who knows all the answers, when his Son gave us assurance: "Be of good cheer." "Do not be afraid." "I will never forsake you!"

The living Christ steadies us when we ask "Why?" He keeps our hearts focused on the God of love and mercy.

Let me relate to you a story about the transforming power of the gospel and our faithfulness as witnesses to it.

More than 200 years ago there was a Quaker preacher who lived in Philadelphia. He was tall, wore a black suit and a broad-brim black hat. Occasionally he would go up the Susquehanna River to Harris Landing, where he would preach. When he went up one trip, he borrowed a horse from friends at the Landing. He had heard there were loggers north of the Landing in virgin forests.

He rode and rode for several hours. Finally, he came to an opening in the forest. The loggers had made a clearing for a crudely built cabin for eating and sleeping. There was a crude fireplace. As Stephen Grellet rode into the opening, he had a strange feeling. He got off his horse, opened the door of the cabin, and concluded that the loggers had abandoned this area and moved on to another. What was he to do? He said, "I have come to preach, so I will preach to an empty cabin." He walked to the front of the fireplace, keeping his hat on, and preached his sermon. That was not the end of the story.

Years later when Grellet was walking across London Bridge, he felt a tap on his shoulder. He stopped, turned around, and a stranger said: "At last I've found thee." Grellet said, "I have never seen thee."

The stranger said, "No, but long ago you came to a logging camp and we had moved on. I left my best axe behind and as I walked nearer to the cabin, I heard a human voice. I walked quietly to the side of the cabin to get my axe where I had left it, and I looked through a hole between the logs and saw you and heard your sermon. When you were through, I quietly left. You never knew that I had been there. And now I have looked for you for fifteen years. At last I've found you, and I want to thank you for that sermon you preached to an empty room. I went back to our new camp and related your sermon. Three of us have become preachers of the gospel. Thank you for your faithfulness."

Eternal one, full of light, lighting every sun and star that reflects its secret: In the light that comes from your grace, let me walk and bask that I may reflect your grace before those who live in darkness of doubt, fear, or unbelief.

Notes

[1]Robert Browning, "Rabbi Ben Ezra," *Anthology of the World's Best Poems*, vol. 4, selected by Edwin Markham (New York: Wm. H. Wise Co, 1950), 1965.

[2]Author unknown.

[3]David E. Browning, *Auburn Reflections*, 2002, 23.

[4]William Wordsworth, "Ode: Intimations of Immortality from Recollections of Early Childhood," *English Romantic Poets*, ed. Stephens, Beck, and Snow (New York: American Book Co., 1952), 62.

A Religion Worse Than None

Exodus 20:3

(October 19, 1947)

The third commandment is most pertinent to contemporary life. It hits us the hardest where life is the weakest. We have developed a technique for avoiding body blows of this century by telling ourselves it is concerned with minor sin, a mere peccadillo. But it refers to something more than a minor sin of profanity. It says something to those who are ashamed to get excited about the living God and his purpose in history. It speaks to those who believe in God and the Christian religion and yet do nothing about it. It condemns a mild anemic religion.

"Thou shalt not take the Lord's name in vain." That means you shall not take up the name of the Lord without a sense of urgency, conviction, and passion.

A religion worse than none is to pay lip service to moral standards but not take them seriously; to think that an intellectual atheism is not dangerous.

A final rejection outright in faith is not yet a present danger, but the acceptance of it in a lifeless way, reserved only for Sunday in a much more pressing danger. This morning I am going to talk about two things: first, what a half-hearted obedience to this commandment has brought about and second, what is the alternative that propels a learning civilization.

We have broken ourselves on the "lost commandment" of the twentieth century. We have taken up the name of God without sincere urgency, while on the other hand we have been passionately busy about other matters, so busy until we have seen religion pushed to the periphery of life. We took up the names of science, education, mammon, progress, nationalism—and worked night and day. And God? We wore him as a label in our suit of social respectability. Of these pursuits—not mentioning science, mammon got our best attention. We have been busy with gold, oil, and world markets. I read about a woman who bet a million dollars on a fur coat in Texas. We are busy making comfortable our homes while letting our churches run down. We are busy piling up our personal resources and parading up and down the avenue of selfishness while we tipped God for foreign missions. While the hungry in the world are crying for bread and good news, we had our fling at a Coney Island view of life.

We sent our missionaries with our pennies, and we kept our dollars—all the while pushing our missionaries into the role of imposters. Listen to this confession of a missionary:

> The world may owe a tremendous debt to the missionary movement. In my heart, however, I feel that missionaries have passed the peak of their usefulness for years to come. They must await a spiritual revival in America. This is more sorely needed than money to carry on the work. The advent of American movies in the Far East turned the tide against us. Up to that time the people were willing to take our word for the character and intelligence of the American people. True, tourists and traders shattered the dream now and then, but they were rare. In general the population of China and Japan took our word. We had the problem of effecting a compromise between the ideal and the real. We had Jesus. Then the movies came, and with the movies the cat leapt out of the bag. The Chinese saw what the Americans are really like, what we are at heart. The movies had exhibited the English-speaking races given over to pleasure, vice, and extravagance. Murderers, gangsters, and cowboys left no further room for further doubt or further deceit. Then followed the radio, and in the wake of the radio, missionaries are left in the role of imposters. The final blow fell with World War II. The East is completely disillusioned. The Russians have made the most of this . . . the struggle for the soul of the Orient lies between them. We are no longer a factor. Our money does not count. . . . The missionary movement may revive . . . but not until something happens to the people here at home.

Without a sense of conviction and urgency the church has drifted along, content to let Caesar have a riotous inning while we sat down to contemplate a future heaven, ignored the God of the Bible, and ran after a dissolved, dissected God defined as a conservator of values, a safety deposit box for moral coupons. We fell in love with the bifurcation of life into the secular and sacred. I'd like to say something about two of these.

First, note that we have let Caesar have his prolonged inning while we have been daydreaming of a future heaven. A church that abandons human affairs renounces the right to call itself Christian. It can keep on talking, but let it not drag the name of the Galilean into the conversation. There looms before the church the evils of war, nationalism, the gross evils of a capitalism that makes for the exploitation of the poor, the problem of racial prejudice, and others. And the moment the church flirts in a compromising way with these forces in order to save its neck, she loses her virtue.

We have tripped into the hammock of heaven-dreaming on the theological rock of "eternal life." We have come to let religion mean our concern about the state of life after death. "I've got religion." "Hail, I'm saved." "I'm heaven bound." Is this the picture?

- You'll have an eight-cylinder car in heaven, air conditioning, indirect lighting, a tile bathroom, and a porcelain kitchen.
- Despite the phenomenal growth of the population, there will be no traffic problem.
- If you would drive out to the Garden of Eden for the weekend, oh the celestial sundaes—all flavors made with the purest chemicals.
- No strike, no speed-up, no layoff
- Everybody a coupon clipper in heaven
- Living in peace on the eternal drudgery of the damned
- All will be fragrant and quiet in heaven, like the best real estate in Westchester, all noise and stench segregated to the underside of the railroad.
- In heaven, when you want something, you just fill out an order and your want is like magic.
- From the power plants, assembly rooms, factories, presses, forges, mines, mills, smelteries, and blast furnaces of hell

And in the same way we have split up life. The biblical view of religion and our contemporary view do not match. The biblical view of religion depicts life not in parts but in its wholeness. But that is not what we have done with religion and life. In this area or in that area we do not let our religion pervade. If you look about you, you will see many evidences of religion, but religion is assigned as a segment. The newspapers have a religious column, stores have religious counters, and publishing companies have a religious department. Should Jesus return, he would want to know why the whole paper was not religious? Why not the whole store?

Religion is not believing certain ideas and doing particular acts. Religion is not a segment of life but the whole, the organization of the whole of it. Someone said that if the Jews had played baseball, you would be able to find the rules of the game in the Book of Leviticus. God is concerned with all that man does, and we all should take God into thought in all we do. Instead, we are void of religious enthusiasm and enemies to spirituality. Do we wonder that religion has been pushed to the edge of life? What are we to do?

There are four fundamental positions or alternatives at our disposal. One is an open rejection of our faith and the acceptance of some pagan system based on the doctrine of race, like the Nazis. Second, we could take the official position of Russia. Third, we could reject the paganism of the Nazis and the atheistic materialism of the Communists, but accept the Christian religion, not as the breath of life, but to maintain the position of respectability. Many of our real convictions are as pagan as those of Nazis: It is the American way. Fourth, we can join the glorious communion of the unashamed, those who will go beyond a mild religion. We cannot be saved until our faith becomes a living force. A tottering civilization cannot be propped up with a weak faith.

Stanley High has reminded us that the church has failed in one great watchword: redemption. This watchword has to be recovered. Our watchword must be love, sacrifice, and devotion. If the church is a fellowship of redeemed sinners dedicated to Christ, its watchword can be none other. The church's spirit must be that of controlled fire. We must get away from a cold intellectualism, but we should not go so far as to become fiery in temper and devouring one another like some lukewarm Protestants who are brought to a boiling point when they see dangers from the Roman Catholic Church or like a "fighting parson" who can stir up a crowd anytime.

Instead, we want a rekindling of the emotions, not by hate and intolerance for others outside the ranks of Christendom. Paul, through the years, was transformed from a destructive flame to a meditating glow of love for those about him. Our enthusiasm will be marked by gentleness and moderation. We will not try to solve the race problem overnight, or the liquor traffic, and the many problems that need the attention of the American people. We can keep about our business with calmness and assurance of our position, just like the scientist S. B. Morse did waiting for congressional action on his invention. Time was on his side, and is on the side of the Christian church as well. Time is on our side. "He that believeth shall not be in haste" (Isa. 28:16).

Two pictures I leave with you:

On the Dartmouth College campus there is a mural satirizing modern education. It depicts a skeleton giving birth to another skeleton. It depicts dry bones creating dry bones. The college professors are portrayed as proceeding to their unrealistic teaching while behind them the world is going up in flames. Change the picture and place the church in the mural against a burning world. The image is now one of a church dragging itself through a lifeless routine of indifference to what is happening in the world. Now what is the answer to that picture?

Picture a man hanging on a cross. His background shows a burning world in every generation. Hugh Miller has reminded us that we say to things: "It was determined that no Caesar should be God, Rome should pass, and the *Aeneid* of Virgil, bravely concocted to be a Roman Bible, should never be more than a school boy's tedium." That is for certain. But the man depicted on the cross . . . there is no lack of urgency or conviction in his life or death. He had not taken the name of God in vain. There is our example in shedding the dirty rags of a religion that is worse than none.

The Voice of Little Men
Exodus 2:23-24, 3:8

"The Voice of Little Men" is the voice of "we the people" and comes to us in recorded form in the Old Testament:

> And the children if Israel sighed by reason of the bondage, and they cried, and their cry came up unto God by reason of the bondage. And God heard their groaning and God remembered his covenant with Abraham, and Isaac, and with Jacob. . . . I have heard their cry . . . and I am come down to deliver them . . . and to bring them out of that land into a good land. (Exod. 2:23)

What a parallel to the cry today of little men everywhere who are denied their God-given freedom. In a world where totalitarian forces would enslave all humanity, their voices are raised in opposition; the voice of little men, whose voice is the cry for freedom. It is that voice . . . so universal and inalienable . . . that unites all the free nations of the earth in the common, sacred cause of keeping alive freedom for all people.

When the rubble of totalitarian war machines, the haranguing of dictators, the constant offer and talk of peace when there is no peace, when all of this clamor would smother the cry of the little man for his place in the sun to live as a free person . . . we who believe in the Christian, democratic way of life must reassure ourselves and the world that freedom is man's right. And God will hear the cry and deliver. In our day we must prize freedom as a precious pearl of great price, and make every sacrifice to keep it alive in the world for others. No sacrifice, however great, is adequate payment for the glorious heritage that is ours by virtue of those who sacrificed that we might have it.

Someday the world will learn that man is free, and that he who sets himself against the freedom of man hurls himself foolishly against the truth that this freedom is a divine principle. The reverence that Jesus had for human personality becomes the anvil that wears away those who exploit and enslave humanity. The awful truth of history is staggering in its testimony of the futility of ignoring this inalienable right of man.

Man is free and was not meant to be a slave for the benefit of a government. That is a lie. . . . And so the fall of colonial Britain.

Man is free and must not be owned by another. . . . And so fell slavery in America.

Man is free and must not be owned by a Hitler or a Mussolini. . . . And so fell Germany's socialism and Italy's fascism.

Man is free. . . . And someday Communism will fall, for it is based on a philosophy that is a lie about economic determinism, bread, and man.

Man is free. . . . It is written in the stars, in the soul of man, and in God's purpose in history.

This glorious dignity of freedom is not without its beauty and clarity. There is no debate about its meaning. It is all-inclusive. We believe in the freedom of religion, conscience, work, press, and one's opinion. We long for freedom from fear, want, and oppression. But all are contained in the word freedom. It is an Anglo-Saxon word meaning "all in the family."

The implications of the doctrine of freedom are far-reaching: "All men, regardless of countless diversities in background, disposition, and achievement, belong to one natural group," . . . therefore no one has a right or destiny that is not characteristic to others. "All men are equally entitled to that which enables them to exercise the functions of being of their kind." Each man—or woman—must be recognized to be deserving of human shelter and clothing and food, of an opportunity to grow, feel, think, know, and have protection against disease and unnecessary pain. This recognition is a guarantee of the right of every man to live and act in ways characteristic of what it means to be human. Each man is unique, with a value all his own—a responsible person, a conscious being. He has a dignity and worth intrinsically as important and as deserving of respect as any other.

A person has the right to worship, enjoy, judge, and believe by himself and to own his own responsibility. No organization ought to demand of any person to view the decision of another as more precious than his own.

A person has the right to pursue any vocation open to others, the place of each being determined not on the basis of race, creed, color, or merit. "All have a right to an equality of opportunity to exhibit their abilities and individuality." This is the good land into which God would have all his children come: the right to food and shelter, growth, health, reason, conscience, and responsibility, private worship and moral decision, social intercourse and leisure, familial life and freedom and justice, and sympathy, education, inquiry, religious activity, and work.

God help our democracy to achieve this good life for our people and all people. Will the little men of the earth be heard? Will all the sons of earth come to know the freedom God has intended? God has heard and is hearing.

> Someday:
> Surely by will, he will blow clear
> His trumpets that all ears shall hear.
> And helping angels shall sweep near,
> And bright banners of the soul advance,
> Up, out of hate and ignorance, into a new inheritance.

We must come to understand that nations have a stewardship over their heritage. Our heritage is the heritage of freedom. That in itself is carrying with it an attendant obligation and responsibility.

Four hundred and fifty years ago everywhere in Europe, the little man began crying anew for his place in the sun of freedom. He was tired of that which denied him the dignity of freedom. In the north, Martin Luther hammered away in his rough German to tell Germans about Christ. In France, Abelard and his teachings were telling in their effectiveness. And in England there came a Cromwell, a Wesley, a Shaftesbury. But man could not come into his own in Europe. So, God, in his providence, opened a new country to the astounding gaze of man where a new life was possible, where freedom's seed would be planted and nourished. It is here in America that man's freedom has flowered as at no other time in history.

In America, the seed sprang into the ideal of a free church in a free state. And from that perspective, it found its way into the American Constitution, which recognized no established creed.

That is our glorious heritage, which, in these dark days when freedom of mankind is being threatened, should inspire us to keep our nation free and the world free. America has become the righteous symbol of "liberty and justice for all." But never, oh never, let us forget the voice of the little men: "We the people"—for the rubbish heap of nations is tragically high.

What can we do to keep freedom's light burning in our own community and in our nation? What can we do to keep America spiritually strong to fulfill her stewardship? We must remember that our own personal freedom must be a disciplined freedom and a responsible freedom.

- We are not free to exploit others.
- We are not free to vent our hate and prejudice on others.
- We are not free to deny others their God-given rights.
- We are not free to deny others justice.

We can begin right there! Justice—which is all inclusive—is justice to the Negro, Jew, employer, employee, Roman Catholic, Protestant, and foreign-born. Freedom is justice for all men. It is absolute. Marshall Field III, declared:

> Freedom is more than a word. Freedom is action, for the foes of freedom never hesitate to take action when they, in their toughness, think that free men are weak. The days ahead will always be filled with peril for freedom, but we can keep freedom if we want it and are vigilant for it. "We the people" must be a living force, not just a phrase to beguile us at political rallies. Man has little stature set against a Norris Dam or measured against a flying fortress, and he will indeed be a small thing unless he decides that his spirit can master the engines of his creation so that his state will be a living force concerned with the freedom of every individual.[1]

We can tone down our repudiation of false gods more positively and affirm our faith in and loyalty to the true God. There is a price to pay to be able to live up to the principle of the worth of every human being. That price is in moral discipline, communion and prayer, and fellowship with God. The grace and power of God in the human heart are sufficient to enable one to grant others their freedom, rights, and privileges.

We can reaffirm our loyalty and devotion to the Christian church as it seeks to perform its fundamental task in the world. "Thus the church's fundamental task—the proclamation of the true God and his will toward man revealed in Christ," Canon John Barry, rector of Hillsborough

Church, Dublin, Ireland, said, "is also its most essential contribution to the cause of peace and freedom in the world." The gospel proclaims a freedom that no man can take away. "Where the Spirit of the Lord is, there is liberty." We can pray to almighty God that he will hear the voice of little men as he heard the cry of his children long ago. God will hear and will use us if we are willing.

> Upon us this great day today
> Have all the ages come:
> Before the pleadings of the world
> Shall we stand helpless, dumb?
>
> O Christ of God, O Son of Man,
> Awake us from our dreams
> Of ancient good and partial truth
> To trust tomorrow's gleams.

During World War II, T. Z. Koo suffered at the hands of the Japanese when he was imprisoned. He told others that he knew what it meant not to be free, but the one place where he remained free all the time, he declared, was in his heart.

Note

[1] Marshall Field, *Freedom Is More Than a Word* (Chicago: University of Chicago Press, 1945), 16.

The Master Speaks

Hebrews 1:1-2; Revelation 3:20

From all the voices around us, there comes one that is authoritative, positive, and eternal. There are voices proclaiming salvation for the economic world, the political and religious. But there is one voice whose voice must be heard in all areas of life, for he alone is the solution to our problems.

In his lifetime the Master's voice was heard. On the hillsides he revealed the character of the new life. At night, he revealed the gift of eternal life. By the well, he revealed the possibilities of the new life. On the sea, he brought "peace" during a stormy time. Before the tomb of Lazarus, he called: "Arise." He speaks with power over life, nature, death.

Two thousand years have failed to weaken that voice. It has been abused, ridiculed, mocked, and slandered, but through all the changes, hatreds, and prejudices of men comes that voice—clarion, positive, and eternal. The Master speaks today and speaks authoritatively by the cross. He speaks the unchangeable word. He speaks with a promise: Whosoever hears will find life.

The Master speaks to his church. Is the church necessary? Yes, the church is necessary:

- It is the bulwark of freedom, liberty, justice, and equality.
- It is the institution that stands for the right at all times as God interprets right.
- It stands for the glory and purity of the home.
- It stands for the worth of the individual.
- It stands as a guide in a darkened world.
- It proclaims the good news of heaven.
- It points to eternity with God; all other voices point to eternity without God.

The church is necessary, and because it is, Christ speaks that she may equip herself to meet the task that is hers.

The Master speaks and demands that the spirit, the glory, the power, and the meaning of the cross be recaptured. The answer is not found in the swastika nor the hammer and sickle, and not in a form of government or a flag, but the cross. The cross is the symbol and spirit of a conquering Christ in a conquering church. This cross is more than the outer crosses that Rome could erect, as it did in many of them. The cross of which I speak is the cross that was built with him—his whole ethical selfhood, the passionate extension of his soul. This was not a cross that was the sign of defeat. Hate did go into its inception; malice wrought its will upon him; scorn and indifference nailed him there, but there was no defeat in his cross.

His cross was the revelation of an all-subduing power giving dramatic expression to eternal love. Love never seems real until we see it in some tragic experience. It was in that divine drama that God proved his love for man.

This is a cross that magnetizes all who come into contact with it: His thought became ours. His ideals became ours. His purpose becomes ours.

It is a cross whose solitariness produces a mystifying awe. No other power is permitted to rank its equal. It permits no racial barrier to stay its advance.

It is dimensionless: There is no range limit applicable. No height limit is applicable. Nothing that man knows outreaches the cross. We will never comprehend it. No depth limit is applicable; it narrows hell for us.

The cross is timeless. It is at home in every period. I saw the empire of evil splashed and spattered like a wine cup shattered, Sodom like Satan, flat on the floor of the world, and in the distance, I saw a spire like a sword raised in victory. Finally in the end, the cross will triumph over all its foes. This awe-inspiring truth must be the very spirit of the church. If she—the church—hears, she shall live.

The Master speaks to the individual. Do we need to listen to him? What about the staggering strain that is present in the world? Look at medical science. If mental ailments increase in the future as in the past few years, by the year 2,000 there may be no sane person living. Look at the upheaval in the political systems and disillusionment of our moral values. What about those living on the margin of life, seeking things on the fringe? The Master speaks that we may meet the great tests of life victoriously. A discovery made by the British colonial office of the natives in equatorial Africa spoke about the natives' response to the desert that was encroaching on them and their response to it. For us, life is often like a great desert ever moving in upon us and testing us.

The first test is to keep our hopes tied up with God. Paul rested his hope in God so that he would not be let down when the crisis of life came. Our hope has to do with the quality of life rather than the circumstances in which we find ourselves. What are you hoping for? Is it a better job? Is it some personal achievement or financial goal or material possession? What is your standard of success for your children?

Christ argues for those hopes that come from the soul. To achieve this hope, somehow we must be anchored outside ourselves to the purpose of God. We often get so tied up with ourselves that we forget God has a plan for us. We are sorry bits of creation when we tie life into knots with our selfishness and stubbornness. Did life turn out for Jesus as he planned it? He seemed sure in the temple as a young child, but ten years got in the way of his plans. But plans changed for him, and the path soon became bitter. But one plan held: They laid a cross on his back. He waited until the nails were driven into his hands and feet and the clouds drifted over his spirit, then he knew . . . "Into thy hands." He was fulfilling God's purpose.

The second test is to keep our faith anchored securely in a hostile world. The world is made hostile by sin, greed, racial riots, competition. When the world seems to be against us, the dice are not loaded in our favor, what then? Do we flee or face the situation? Or do we turn to those inner, spiritual resources that can sustain us? Do we find that solid hope that can sustain us?

The Master stands and speaks. Holman Hunt painted a picture of Jesus standing before the door of our heart and knocking for entrance. You may be alone on your own island of selfhood, and you will hear no splash of a friendly oar coming toward you, if you do not want it. You may barricade yourself in the mountain fortress of your own personality and need dread no invitations. You may sit alone in the unlighted chambers of your soul, and the Savior will take no unbidden step across your threshold. You must respond. He will not force himself upon you.

But he speaks: "I stand at the door and knock."

Christianity Confronts Communism

Matthew 7:15-16

(February 26, 1950)

Brig. Gen. C. T. Lanham of the U.S. Army has this to say about our great ideological argument for our way of life:

> It is the argument of the American bathroom. Our soldiers are politically illiterate and are no match for the sophisticates of Europe. When they are driven into an intellectual corner they will turn for the defense to our millions of radios, televisions, automobiles and the American bathroom. It is unfortunate that we are no more skillful advocates of the philosophy we live by . . . not that we will become converted to other ways of life . . . but the people of Europe are bewildered by men who appear indifferent to political and philosophical bases of the most powerful nation on earth. Furiously we have concentrated our efforts on stark materialism. We have neglected our spiritual needs.

Such an argument is mere straw in staying the ruthless and ever-growing tide of a totalitarian way of life—Communism. An indifference to our spiritual heritage and the neglect of our spiritual deeds make us a sure target for the forces of evil so effectively organized.

It is straw because the argument that prevails in the long run is the spiritual one.

Everywhere men are searching for the answer to Communism; they are searching for the one argument that will prevail over the advocates of force.

There is only one answer and one argument: Christianity. The total answer is as strong as the individual Christian answers. Every Christian is confronted with terrible responsibilities during these ominous days.

Concerning my Christian faith, I am faced with these questions:

- Am I accepting it in a half-hearted manner?
- Am I a good advocate of the Christian way of life?
- When driven to the corner, what does my life say about Christianity?

Concerning Communism, I am faced with these questions:

- Do I understand the philosophy, promises, and methods of Communism?
- Am I wise enough to know what the enemy is at heart?
- Am I aware of what life on earth will become if those enemies of freedom, righteousness, and justice succeed in this generation?

Christianity is confronted with Communism and sees in it a bad philosophy of life. Communism is more than just an economic theory of production for use rather than profit. It is more than a defense of the worker and the disinherited. It is more than a form of collectivism opposed to the individualism of the West. It is a bad philosophy of life.

It is trying to achieve an ideal by un-ideal means that contradict the end that is sought. It oversimplifies the class structure with its division of society into two socially effective groups. It neglects the common patriotic, moral, and religious sentiments and convictions that hold classes together. Its worldview is inadequate, because its mechanistic explanation of the universe is not satisfying. Communism's understanding of human nature is inadequate. Human nature guided by a materialistic philosophy can never rise above hedonism. (Let us eat, drink, and be merry.) It is confined to space and time and thinks of man as purely a natural phenomenon. What is man? Only what he eats!

The abolition of private property is not the solution to the ills of mankind. The desire for aggression can never be eradicated. Its psychology is poor. Marx is really ignorant of the real philosophy of life. The love of money is not the only evil. Men also love power—to boss—which is just as bad. Communism also denies the existence of God. It is at heart a bad philosophy that is expressed in the "beatitudes" of the communistic way of life. We not only face a bad philosophy of life in Communism, but also a godless religion whose devotees are afire with zeal and fervor.

Someone has said that as Christians we must outlive them. We must show more faith, zeal, courage, daring, sacrifice, understanding, and concern for the underprivileged. We must beat them to the punch every time. Their interest, zeal, and passion are not to be underestimated. They are fired with a passion that will not quibble over comforts, money, ease, sacrifice, or death.

As Christianity confronts Communism today, it is aware of a remarkable demonstration of the transforming power of faith. An enfeebled Christendom is facing a demonstration of faith by those who deny God. The power of faith in a false ideal is real. We have to acknowledge that one of the dynamic forces in all achievements is faith. Life has been made worth living for the millions of disinherited people by the fact of faith in what has been promised and the cause for which they have given themselves. The tragedy for the twentieth century is that so many have demonstrated faith in a false ideal. What if all that faith was centered in the truth: Christ? Christianity confronts Communism—in spite of motive, means, and error—with an essentially corrective finger. This may seem to be absurd, but I believe the facts are precisely true.

Communism is a secularized version of a strain of the Hebrew prophets. It gets its social passion and justice from the Bible. Communism got the idea of the "coming of age" from the Revelation of John. Communism identifies its goal with a new age and society. It has been pointed out that Communism is a response to one-sidedness in the development of the churches. Communism has acted as a reminder of the response of Christians and the church to seek social justice and equality.

"What is the cause of this atheistic communism?" Jacques Maritain asks. "It is, I believe, because at the origin of Communism, and above all owing to the fault of a Christian world unfaithful to its principles, there lies a profound sense of resentment against the Christian world, and not only again the Christian world, but—here is the tragedy—against Christianity itself."[1]

Nicolas Berdyaev has reminded us of the responsibility Christians have to accept for their contribution to the uprising of Communism:

Christians who condemn Communism cannot lay whole blame upon these godless Communists; they must assign part of the blame to themselves and that is a considerable part. They must also be penitents. Have Christians done much for the realization to Christian justice in social life? Have we striven to realize the brotherhood of man? The sins of historical churches have been great . . . and these sins bring with them just punishment.[2] If the laboring classes have become exceptionally favorable breeding ground for the poison of godlessness, if militant atheism has become nothing less than the opium of the people, the guilt must be attributed first of all by no means to the agitators of revolutionary socialism, but also to the Christians, to the whole Christian world. It is not Christianity, of course, that is to blame, but Christians: they are too often pseudo-Christians.[3]

We have been looking at the enemy of righteousness in our discussion of Communism; let us turn our thoughts to the Christian faith. What are some valuable lessons of truth for us as we seek to make our Christianity more telling?

We must learn the art of self-criticism that is encouraged by Christian humility. That is good Christian strategy and good Christianity! Humility is the major corrective to distorted judgment. Our judgments usually come from the narrow interests of the group in which we move. We must cultivate the habit of seeing everything under God's criticism. That will take the poison out of all relations, private or international. That would help break the vicious circle of self-righteous denunciation between Russian and Anglo-Saxon nations. Christians must always begin with their own sins rather than the sins of their opponents.

No solution is adequate for the ills of the world unless a future is guaranteed for all people. This guarantee has to be for those of all creeds and races. Christian love must seek the welfare of all. The actual content of obedience to God means the subordination of private interests and narrow group interests for the good of all. To seek to do the will of God in our concrete situation is to seek the good of all his children. Our social passion and compassion must go further than our own interests. If bread is on my table, then there must be bread for all. We must ever be on the lookout for new revelations of God. We miss those revelations when we identify God too closely with any ideal, institution, denomination, economic theory, or political philosophy.

As a Christian, what can I do in this conflict? We need to see in Communism a peril, yes, but to see in it a great challenge to Christianity. The appeal comes to Christians to live up to the test of their faith. "By their fruits ye shall know them." If there is disorder, we are challenged to add leaven of straight thinking, moral integrity, and hope for victory of righteousness. Injustice in our society challenges us to be just in all actions. Tyranny challenges us to resist with good works. We are challenged to resist the powers of evil with spiritual forces. We will never stop any force of evil by arm-waving, smearing, and raising a hysterical voice.

If the world lacks love, we are challenged to give it love. If the world lacks light, we are to give it light. If the world lacks hope, we are to give it hope.

Evil is put on the run by the positive force of good of Christians everywhere. Let us work for the strengthening of the Christian church. "Men and women who have spiritual faith and who want also to do something practical to preserve peace and to meet the challenge of communism," John Foster Dulles said, "have in their church the most effective medium that exists." Christianity must show some consecrated loyalty, sacrificial devotion, passion for emancipation, some intense belief in its own cause as do the Communists in their cause. The claim of Christ is exacting. If Christianity is going to make a difference in the battle against Communism, its devotion and loyalty to the church must be without question.

Live your life in obedience and leave the future with God. Look at the time image Sir James Jeans depicts for us. The height of a TV tower equals the time passed since earth formed.

Climb a tower and place a Coke cap on top of the tower. That thickness represents the time man has been on earth. Place a safety razor on top of the cap, which represents the recorded history of man. On the razor blade place gold foil 7/10,000 inch in thickness, which represents the duration of God's revelation of Christianity.

Other forces will rise, but in each age a bit of gold foil will be added. And a day will come when it will reach heaven and God's will will be done on earth.

Notes

¹Jacques Maritain, *Integral Humanism: Temporal and Spiritual Problems of a New Christendom* (Notre Dame: University of Notre Dame Press, 1973), 41.

²Nicolas Berdyaev, *The Origin of Russian Communism* (London: Geoffrey Bles: The Centenary Press, 1937), 207-208.

³Nicolas Berdyaev, *The Russian Revolution* (Ann Arbor: University of Michigan Press, 1961), 89.

(This sermon, according to Browning, was requested by Theodore Rankin of the Foreign Mission Board, Richmond, Virginia, who was present when it was preached.)

This Is My Body

1 Corinthians 11:24

(October 5, 1948)

These words, "This is my body," have led to dissension within the church, the body of Christ. These words have caused angry words and sword laid on those within the church. "This is my body." And blood, innocent blood, shed over one's interpretation of them . . . what do they mean?

What if Jesus had been the greatest musician who ever lived? If his singing and playing the harp were a combination of all that we know of Mozart and Bach and Beethoven? Multitudes, thousands, were always gathering to hear Jesus as he set up his stage—no lights or strobes. The crowds would go wild, always calling for more.

And what if he was coming to the end of his career, even prematurely, would he have gathered his most ardent and capable followers into a room for a last meal with them? Would he have said, "This music is my body; eat it"? Would the disciples have gone into the world believing that their music would convert people?

Music thrills and calms the soul, but it is not redemptive. Had his disciples gone throughout the known world repeating the music of Jesus, would that have been the way of salvation? Would that music have called for repentance and renewal? Music is not a moral issue; man's condition before God is moral. And to be reconciled to God takes more than what music can do. In music, however beautiful and calming and uplifting, one does not have the Isaiah experience in the temple: "Woe is me, for I am undone."

On that night when he ate the Passover supper with disciples, Jesus said, "This is my body; take and eat." What did he mean? Did he mean there was a way, led by the proper person, that the host was transformed into the flesh of Jesus? Which is of greater value to the Christian, the earthly body of Jesus or the living, resurrected Christ?

Or was Jesus saying something different? . . . "Here you see me in the flesh, knowing all that I stood for and taught. I want you to 'eat me'; that is, let all I said and did become a part, the whole of your life. I will be enough for you to carry on my work of redemption. Have I not said 'I am the bread of life; I am the water of life'? Take me into your life, and I will sustain you as bread and water sustain your life."

Why did Jesus say "This is my body" at the meal rather than after the crucifixion? The historical Jesus' life at this point was incomplete. The cross lay ahead. And until that experience took place, the "body" of Jesus was incomplete. Jesus told them he would be crucified. But they could not comprehend the meaning of the cross, and some probably didn't believe he would be crucified. He did not eat with his disciples and say "this is my body" after the resurrection.

He told his disciples to "remember him." And that is the point of his talk with his disciples.

You need to "remember me" when you have the supper again, for you are to carry on my work and teachings. And you will gain courage and the will to be faithful, if you remember and take me into your pilgrimage. And later he told his disciples, after the resurrection, "I will send the Holy Spirit to strengthen you, guide you, and keep you alert to me— and my earthly life with you."

Surely we need to come together in worship and communion, for there is much to take our minds off Jesus and his calling. But do the bread and wine become the body of Jesus, or do they remain bread and wine until eaten and drunk?

By faith we believe that when we are partaking of the elements, we have faith that Christ is with us in the act of faith—not in the bread and wine. In faith as we eat bread and drink wine, he is remembered and our responsibility made more imperative. And in that faith, the living Christ—not the historical Jesus—comes to be with us. That hour of remembrance sends us forth to let the spirit, mind, and faith of Jesus consume us and strengthen us for discipleship.

Approach the rose in all wonder and awe. It does not take its beauty and aroma lightly. It is serious about what it is and who made it. Look with deep attention and accept its beauty—there to bless.

Woodrow Wilson Hasty
(Pastor, 1950-1964)

Woodrow Wilson Hasty was the tenth child born to Charlie and Maude Maddrey Hasty on May 17, 1919, in Jackson, North Carolina. Woody Hasty spent his early life in Jackson, and after graduation went on to Wake Forest College (now University) and graduated with a B.S. in history and political science. He graduated from Crozer Theological Seminary in Chester, Pennsylvania, with a B.D. degree and later did graduate study in homiletics at Union Theological Seminary in New York City. In recognition of his ministry, he was awarded an honorary Doctor of Divinity degree by Keuka College in Keuka Park, New York.

Hasty married the former Jane Aller Squire of Mt. Vernon, New York, and they had two children and one grandson.

He began his ministry as assistant pastor at First Baptist Church in Mt. Vernon, New York, and became pastor of Kings Highway Baptist

Church in Brooklyn, New York, in 1946. After a short tenure there, he became pastor of Wallace Baptist Church in Wallace, North Carolina.

On November 1, 1950, Hasty accepted a call to be the second pastor of River Road Church, Baptist, and continued his ministry with the church until mid-June 1964. Under his distinguished ministry, the church grew in membership to more than a thousand members. The facilities were expanded from the existing chapel to the construction of the fellowship house, the second of the three phases of the church's physical plant. He was also actively involved with the students and faculty at the nearby University of Richmond, especially the Baptist Student Union.

Reflecting on his years of ministry at River Road Church following his death, Connie Showalter, a member of the church's history committee, wrote in *The Spire* on October 23, 2003, of Dr. Hasty:

> [He] had the gift for dealing with complex theology with a simple touch. He was clear and direct and personal. . . . He had an uncommon ability to reach the common man in the pew. However, he preached no common message. He was conversant with the most current theological thinking and was able to explain and interpret the traditional symbols and rituals of worship.

From Richmond, Hasty became senior minister of Scarsdale Community Baptist Church in Scarsdale, New York, serving from 1964-1970. From 1970-1975, he served as senior minister of Seabreeze United Church in Daytona Beach, Florida, where the church plant was enlarged and the attendance and outreach of the church expanded. He later served as senior minister at the historic Plymouth Congregational Church in Miami, Florida, from 1975 until his retirement in 1990. During his ministry, the church membership grew from 900 to more than 3,000, and the church was recognized by the United Church of Christ Biennial Conference in 1987 for the fastest growth in the denomination nationwide. After retiring, Dr. Hasty served as interim pastor in Naples, Florida, and Wayzata, Minnesota, before returning to Richmond and uniting as a member of River Road Church again. In 2002 he and his wife returned to Naples, Florida, where he once again served as interim associate minister of the Naples United Church.

On September 23, 2003, Woodrow Hasty died in Naples at the age of eighty-four.

A Dangerous Book

2 Timothy 3:1-17

(December 9, 1962)

I hold in my hand a book we call the Bible. It has not always been called the Bible. That name was not attached to it until about the fifth century A.D. This book breaks the silence of the dawn with the magnificent words, "In the beginning God." It hushes the world to sleep with the prayer, "The grace of our Lord Jesus Christ be with you all." On the very first page we hear the voice of God saying, "Let there be light." As the book draws to a close, we hear the truth of God proclaiming, "Let there be life." All through this book there are warnings so clear and so commanding that the wicked and the proud are made to tremble, but for the humble and the penitent it has a mother's voice. From this book we get guidance for our lives. In it we find comfort and a companion for the lonely heart. Through it we hear God speaking to us.

This book was not dictated by God. It was not written by any one man during a lifetime. Rather, it was written by a whole host of men over a period of approximately twelve hundred years. It was not written by a host of literary geniuses such as Euripides, Plato, and Shakespeare. It was written by shepherds, lawgivers, kings, prophets, priests, poets, fishermen, and Christian missionaries. Yet, there are lines in it that deserve to be carved in granite. It was written by men whose minds were inspired and whose hearts were God-shaped, and through their words God still speaks. We call this book the Word of God then, not because God dictated it, but because it was written by men whose minds were inspired by God and whose hearts were God-shaped, and because God is still able to speak to you and me through these men's words. This book, when rightly interpreted and imaginatively read, is as fresh as this morning's newspaper. Yet, it is as old-fashioned and dependable as grandfather's walking stick.

Since this is Universal Bible Sunday, I would like for us to think together about this grand old book that many of you first heard as you stood at your mother's knee or as you sat in your father's lap.

The book we call the Bible had its beginning many centuries before Christ as the lawgivers and priests, prophets and kings and poets of the Hebrew people put down their history, their record of God's dealing with them, and their inspired insights and hopes. Because those writings were part of the very life of the Hebrew people, they were copied and recopied many times, for household and temple and synagogue, in generation after generation.

By the time of Jesus, these sacred writings were gathered into three groups known as "the Law," "the Prophets," and "the Writings." The group known as the Law consisted of what we now know as the first five books of our Bible. The group known as the Prophets consisted of the works of Isaiah, Jeremiah, Ezekiel, and the twelve Minor Prophets. The group known as the Writings consisted of Psalms, Proverbs, Job, etc. It was these—the Law, the Prophets, and the Writings—on which Jesus nourished his soul.

Some of those early books were written on scrolls made out of dried reeds growing in the mud at the river's edge. This material was called "papyrus." Other early books were written on material made from the skins of animals. All of them were written in the Hebrew language.

Once the Christian church came into existence, other writings began to appear. Paul, the apostle, began to write some letters to the little groups of people in various cities who had come to believe the gospel he preached to them. As these groups received the letters, they were treasured and carefully preserved. Soon neighboring churches wanted copies, and thus Paul's letters began to circulate. The need of teaching new converts and for continuing the witness of the first disciples to the life and teachings of our Lord led to the writing of the Gospels with their priceless testimony to Jesus. Other letters, exhortations, sermons, and similar Christian writings also came into circulation.

All of these Christian writings—Paul's letters, the Gospels, and the like—were also first written on sheets of papyrus or skins of animals. The writing was done with pens made from reeds, and the ink was usually made from fish oil and soot.

Can't you see in your mind's eye little groups of Christians, when it was not popular to be a Christian, gathered around the bonfires or huddled underneath the crimson ripple of the torchlight, or scrounged up in a cave somewhere listening to someone read from one of their scrolls? If the scroll contained one of Paul's letters, it no doubt brought back memories of his stay in their midst. If the scroll contained a part of the gospel, it must have brought back memories of green fields, wild flowers, and those deep, caressing eyes of the young man from Galilee. How those early Christians did cherish their sacred scrolls! How eagerly they listened to someone read them!

Let us return for a moment to our story of the development of the book we call the Bible. To make a long story short, let me say that the writings on scrolls we have spoken of were, by the second century, copied on sheets of skillfully treated animal skins, called "vellum" or "parchment," and sewn together in book form. After a long period of sifting the wheat from the chaff, the books that were thought worthy of such a place were all bound together and called the Bible, a word that etymologically viewed means "the books" or "a library." The Bible is really a library of many books under one cover.

This book, the Bible, was eventually translated into Latin and finally into English. That is a long story. It is a long story because the powerful church leaders wished to keep the people in ignorance and fought against translating the Bible into the languages the common people could read and understand.

As for the Bible in English, it was not translated until about 600 years ago, and then it was printed and read in situations so dangerous that we can scarcely credit the stories that have come down to us. Yet, there is little doubt that those stories are true. Englishmen who worked to translate the Bible in the language of the people were burned at the stake with their Bibles tied around their necks. The church hunted to their death those who possessed this book. John Wycliffe, the famous translator, was fortunate in that he died a natural death, but in futile, ferocious revenge, his body was dug up and burned and the ashes scattered.

A hundred years later, William Tyndale, a man of only thirty years of age, crossed to the Continent in order to found an underground movement for the printing of the Bible in English so that every English plowboy could read it. He became an exile never to see his homeland again.

He shipped his Bibles to England hidden in bales of cotton, in bundles of flax, and in bags of flour. The books were eagerly bought, although the church did everything to destroy them, punished those who were found possessing them, and tried to stop their import. Finally, Tyndale himself was imprisoned near Brussels and subsequently strangled to death and his body burned to ashes. Four hundred years ago this young man of only forty-two laid down his life so that we might have the Bible in our own tongue.

You see, then, this Bible I hold in my hand—bound in attractive cover, printed on thin and high-grade paper, and translated into the English language—has a long history. From huge scrolls of papyrus and large stacks of animal skins upon which men, a host of them, wrote their highest thoughts, their keenest insights, and a record of God's dealing with them, we have this thin and readable Bible. From the Hebrew and Greek languages we have it in the idiom of our day. In days when it was dangerous to be a Christian, men gathered in secret hideaways to read it. In days when it was dangerous to translate it in languages men could read, men still did it. In one sense of the word, this book has been for some in days past a dangerous book. Strange as it may sound, it is in some ways for some people a dangerous book today. Let me explain,

The Bible is a dangerous book for you if you want to live an idle, complacent life and do nothing to make your world better. One man put it like this:

> When I read the Bible I sometimes feel that I am in the theater enjoying a marvelous drama as the events unfold before my eyes. But then and again it seems that God interrupts the drama with the announcement: "Is John Smith in the house?" And I am John Smith. Then God says: "Report immediately for a task intended for you alone!" Have you ever heard God speak to you as you read the Bible? Sure you have. I have. Through it he will call to you. And before you know it, you will be saying with Isaiah of old, "Here am I, Lord, send me."

The Bible is a dangerous book for you if you think you can do wrong and then run or hide from God. Read your Bible, and the notion that you can run or hide from God will be blasted. In the opening pages of the Bible you will see Adam and Eve—symbols of the first man and woman—crouched behind a tree trying to hide because they know they have done wrong. God comes walking through the garden calling out, "Adam, where art thou?" Adam comes sneaking from behind the tree reluctantly saying, "I heard thy voice and I was afraid." What is the writer of that old, old story saying but this: "You cannot hide from God—no need to try it"? Or again listen to the Psalmist as he says, "Whither shall I flee from thy spirit? If I ascend into the heavens, thou art there. If I make my bed in hell, lo thou art there. If I dwell in the uttermost parts of the sea, thou art there." You can't run or hide from God. But why try it? For the penitent, God has a mother's voice.

The Bible is a dangerous book for you if you feel that you can be at odds with your fellowman and still be in tune with God. Jesus, you know, emphasized the importance of worship. We are told that he himself went to the place of worship on the Sabbath, as was his custom. Yet, there is one place in the Bible where he seems to say there is something even more important than going to church to worship. He says, "If you go to worship and remember that there is something wrong between yourself and another, go and try to make it right. Then come and worship." He seems to say, reconciliation, whenever it is possible, is more important than worship. For you cannot be at odds with men and in harmony with God at the same time.

Then again, if by chance you wish to draw the draperies of despair across your life and keep out all light from the sun and stars, and live in utter darkness, then for you the Bible is a dangerous book. For the truth of the matter is as you read your Bible, hope keeps tucking back the draperies and allowing light to shine in.

In the first chapter of Genesis we read, "And the evening and the morning were the first day." We would not have written it that way. Most of us would have written it: "And the morning and the evening were the first day." Not so in the Bible. It says: "And the evening and the morning were the first day." What does it mean? Simply this: God's day always ends in dawn. The darkness will never in the end triumph. Read the story of Christ's birth, the story of Christmas, and hope will tug at the draperies and allow light to shine in. Read the story of Easter. What incontestable evidence you have here of the ultimate triumph of the purposes of God. Read the Book of Revelation. It's difficult to understand, but it is saying that no atheistic state, no power of darkness will in the end be victorious. God is the supreme ruler of his world. Evil men may hold back his purposes and delay his plan, but they cannot defeat him.

Yes, the person who is uncaring, unkind, unclean, and unconvinced that there is any hope and by some strange quirk wants to remain that way should steer clear of the Bible. For him it is a dangerous book. But the person who may often fall short but who really wants to be decent, clean, and live a worthy life will find in the Bible, guidance, comfort, inspiration, consolation, and hope.

Perhaps you recall seeing the coronation of Queen Elizabeth on television a few years ago, and remember that on that occasion the British Sovereign was presented with a copy of the Bible. You've doubtless forgotten the words used in making the presentation, but they were as follows:

> To keep your Majesty ever mindful of the Law and the Gospel of God as the rule for the whole life and government of Christian Princes, we present you with this Book, the most valuable thing that this world affords. Here is wisdom; this is the Royal Law; these are the lively oracles of God.

"The most valuable thing that this world affords"
—The Bible

On Being a Christian

Acts 11:19-26

(February 10, 1963)

"It was in Antioch that the disciples were first called Christians," so says St. Luke in the Book of Acts. What sort of a place was Antioch? Come with me, if you will, to Antioch and we shall see.

Antioch was located in northern Syria, an area that today is in modern Turkey. It was one of the greatest cities in the Roman Empire. "Antioch, the Beautiful," "The Queen of the East"—by such names it was called. It ranked with Rome and Alexandria as one of the three greatest cities of the Greco-Roman world. Antioch had probably a million inhabitants, including a large Jewish population, and the synagogue there was next to the one in Alexandria, the most magnificent in the world. You see, then, that Antioch was not a crossroad village in some out-of-the-way spot. It was a great city, one of the greatest cities of the Greco-Roman world.

Now let us look at the church that was started in Antioch. Following the stoning of Stephen, a persecution broke out in Jerusalem. To escape the persecution, some followers of Jesus fled as far north as Antioch and there began a little church. When these followers of Jesus began preaching in Antioch, some Gentiles, who had never been Jews, listened. Many were converted and wanted to join the fellowship of the followers of Jesus. How were they to do this? This was the question the young church in Antioch faced when it was barely able to stand on its feet. The mother church in Jerusalem had said that Gentiles desiring to become followers of Jesus must first become Jews and comply with all the Jewish laws, be circumcised and obey all the strict little rules about Sabbath keeping and kosher foods. But the church in Antioch had liberal leaders, men of vision, and they said that if the Gentiles were truly sincere and desired wholeheartedly to be followers of Jesus, then they should open the doors of their fellowship to them. This they did. We might say it was a church with open membership. The church began to grow rapidly. "A great number," says Luke, "believed and turned to the Lord."

News has a way of getting around, you know. So news of what the church in Antioch was doing soon reached the conservative brethren of the Jerusalem church. As you might expect, the Jerusalem church quickly sent a representative to Antioch to see firsthand what was going on. Fortunately the man they chose was Barnabas. What a man he was! He was, as Luke says, "a good man, full of the Holy Spirit and of faith." He was also liberal-minded, sympathetic, and good-natured. When Barnabas reached Antioch, he was delighted with the way the Gentiles were being reached by the gospel and added to the church. Furthermore, he encouraged the liberal attitude the church of Antioch had taken.

Then Barnabas did something that was to have tremendous historic consequences. He traveled eighty miles from Antioch to Tarsus, where Paul the Apostle was then preaching, and persuaded Paul to join him, and together they went to Antioch and became teammates in one of the most important movements in the early church.

It was there in Antioch—in the church that was out of favor with the strict conservatives in Jerusalem—that the disciples were first called "Christians." It may have been a nickname, intended as a derogatory nickname, invented by the enemies of Jesus; we don't know for sure. We do know it was a good name and it stuck. "Christians," partisans of Christ, devoted adherents of Christ—that's what the word meant.

What does it mean to be a Christian today? How can we tell if we are Christians? Is a man a Christian simply by virtue of not being a Muslim or a Buddhist? If so, a hardened criminal might justifiably wear the Christian label. Is a man a Christian simply because he lives according to the Golden Rule? No. Any decent and respectable agnostic may fulfill that condition. What does it mean, then, to be a Christian?

Does the mere fact of having our names on a church roll make us Christians? No, I'm afraid not. It's not that simple. What, then, is a Christian? Let me give you the best answer I have been able to formulate from my experience, my study in seminary, and from all my reading on the subject.

First of all, I would say that a Christian is one who sincerely tries to be a follower of Jesus Christ.

Now some of you may feel that I'm being too lenient or that I'm watering the matter down too much by using the word "tries"—tries to be a follower of Jesus Christ. I have thought this thing through as carefully as I know how, and I feel the word "tries"—sincerely tries—is correct.

Let me put it this way: If you were to ask me if I considered myself a golfer, I would reluctantly say yes—but I'd say it. I sincerely try to play the game. I strive to improve the way I play. I love it. The exercise is good for me, the beauty of the out-of-doors thrills me, the fresh air wipes the cobwebs out of my brain, the crack of the ball against the club and the flight of a well-hit ball give me a feeling that only golfers know. So I would say, if you asked me, that I am a golfer. But if I had to par every hole in order to be a golfer, if I had to execute every swing perfectly, then I'm not a golfer and never will be one.

Again and again when I come home from the golf course, Randy, my seven-year-old son, will ask me if I won. I tell him I won a few holes but not the game. Then one day he said, "Daddy, don't you ever win a game?" I had to say, "Hardly ever, son." Tears came into his eyes and he said, "Daddy, I feel so sorry for you."

I still say I'm a golfer—I try, I sincerely try to play the game. How foolish to say you must par every hole before you can be called a golfer. How very wrong to assume you must be a perfect follower of Christ before you can be considered a Christian. No one succeeds perfectly. The Apostle Paul confessed miserable failure in the Christian life. Quite frankly he wrote to the Philippians, "Brethren, I do not count myself to have succeeded." "But," he added, "I press on . . ." He was sincerely trying. That's one of the things it means to be a Christian. Are you sincerely trying?

Second, in order to be a Christian, one must hold certain convictions about Christ.

After the disciples had tramped the dusty roads of Galilee with Jesus for three years, fished with him in its lake, slept beside him in the open on its gentle hills, broken bread with him by its waysides, and listened rapturously to his teachings in the market places and village greens, they went with him into a quiet spot in Caesarea Philippi. Gathering them around him in an intimate circle, he asked them, "Who do men say that the Son of Man is?"

Promptly came the reply: "Some say John the Baptist; some Elijah; and others Jeremiah, or one of the prophets."

Then he asked them, "But whom say ye that I am?" With a question put to them so personally and so directly, they couldn't help but keep quiet and think hard. Suddenly the silence of their introspection was rent by impulsive, warmhearted Peter: "Thou art the Christ, the Son of the living God." The rest of the disciples had been thinking that, too, but a shyness had muted their tongues. In their hearts they knew it to be true.

For nineteen centuries the church has believed that Jesus of Nazareth, while fully and completely human, revealed in his person, as nothing before or since has ever revealed, was the whole nature of God. We have tried to express that truth by calling him the Christ, the Son of God. We are all created sons of God, but Christ is in some way the unique Son of God. That is why men have followed Jesus and called him Master and Lord, not because he was the cleverest or bravest man who ever lived, but because he had something different about him, something more than human, something divine.

"Thou art the Christ, the Son of the living God." Do you believe that? The reaching of that decision may happen dramatically as it did to Paul on the Damascus Road, or it may happen quietly and slowly as it did to Charles Wesley. He simply felt strangely warmed within. In an ordinary service of worship there came to Wesley the honest conviction, which probably had been forming in his mind for years, that Jesus was in some unique way the Son of God; that he was the Christ, his Saviour. Have you reached any such decision?

Third, if a person is a Christian, he will be the best possible member of Christ's church.

Now I'm not saying that a good man who doesn't belong to the church will not go to heaven. I am willing to leave that matter in the hands of a loving, understanding God.

What I am saying is that a person may at times be impatient with the church's weakness and stodginess, but if he once understands that it is Christ's own creation and not just an optional religious society, he will affiliate with it. When a man sees that whatever has been accomplished in the name of Christ through nineteen centuries has been accomplished not by single piccolos and flutes tooting their little isolated wails, but by the great symphony of the church playing harmoniously under its divine conductor, he will ask no higher privilege than to be a member of that symphony and to play his part, however obscure, in making the church strong and effectual.

Zacchaeus, you remember, was the man who climbed up a tree one day so he could see Jesus. Jesus spied him as he passed along the road, called to him, and went to his house to dine. An old and beautiful legend relates that Zacchaeus, after he had been converted, used to rise early occasionally and leave the house. His wife was curious to know where he went and what he did, so one morning she followed him. (Wives do that sometimes, you know.) At the town well he lowered a bucket, filled it with water, went out through the city gates, and walked until he came to a sycamore tree. There, setting down the bucket of water, he began to cast away the stones and rubbish that lay about the foot of the tree. Having done this, he poured water on the roots of the tree and stood silent as if in affectionate reminiscence and contemplation. When his amazed wife came out of her hiding place and asked what he was doing, Zacchaeus replied, "This is where I found Christ."

For nineteen centuries people have borne that same tender, affectionate witness concerning the church. "This is where I found Christ." Christians will love the church and belong to it. They may be discouraged at its blindness and its slowness, but they will still love it. It is where they found Christ, where they still find him, and where they can labor together with others to carry on his work.

Where did you first find Christ, may I ask? Where did you first meet him? Many of you met him in a similar place to where I met him: in a little village church where the pews were hard, the music atrocious, and where I squirmed throughout the sermon, but where my parents went because they found strength there and where humble and godly church school teachers told me stories I have never forgotten.

I am indebted to the Christian church. It was in the church where I first met Christ. It provided a soil in which my spiritual life could grow. You are indebted to the church, too. You are surrounded on every hand by traditions that came out of the church, by families whose roots are in the church, by institutions and ideals that were born of the church, and by men and women who believe in the church and serve the church. Those who claim to be Christians will know that their place is in the church.

They will eventually find their place in the church, make it better than they found it, and be the best members possible.

Are you associated with the church? I know you are. Are you trying to be the best possible member? A Christian will try.

One day the philosopher Josiah Royce was sitting in his study at Harvard University talking with a young student. In the course of the conversation the student asked the professor, "What is your definition of a Christian?" The great philosopher replied, "I do not know how to define a Christian." But wait," he added, looking out of the window. "There goes Phillips Brooks." That was his definition, a walking definition.

As we make our way home today, could anyone honestly point to us and say, "There goes a Christian"?

Life's Greatest Lesson

Romans 12

(April 28, 1963)

There are many great teachers in the world; men and women who teach with their lives as well as their lips; men and women who know how to capture the attention of students, fire their imaginations, and set the wheels of their minds in rapid motion. If you have ever been privileged to sit at the feet of such a teacher, your life has been greatly blessed and you should be eternally grateful. But of all the great teachers, none is greater than experience or life itself. What have you learned from life? Let me go even farther: What is the greatest lesson life has ever taught you?

If it were possible for us to put this question to the old Psalmist, the one who wrote so many of the Psalms in the Old Testament, he might possibly refer us to Psalm 23 and say, "Read that and you will find running through it the greatest lesson life taught me." If it were possible for us to put the same question to Jesus, he might possibly suggest we read again the Sermon on the Mount, words that fell from his lips as he stood on a Galilean hillside. Then again if we could place before the Apostle Paul the same question, who knows, he might suggest that we read again the twelfth chapter of his letter to the Romans. There in that twelfth chapter the Apostle Paul comes down to earth and writes in a simple way about everyday, practical Christian living. You get the feeling as you read it that the writer is saying: Here are some of the lessons life has taught me. Profit from them; learn from them.

Some years ago—just how many years ago I'm not sure—but some several years ago an Englishman conceived the happy idea of writing to a number of outstanding people of his day and asking them to answer the question, "What is the greatest lesson life has taught you?" Here are four of the brief replies he received:

Sir Oliver Lodge, an outstanding scientist of that day, replied: "The greatest lesson life has taught me is the reality of the spiritual world."

Miss Maude Royden, one of the best-known women preachers of the world, one who had a physical disability and knew constant suffering, replied: "The greatest lesson life has taught me is that all things can work together for good to them that love Christ."

Dr. R. F. Horton, the minister of one of the wealthiest congregations in London, and accustomed to meeting with people of considerable means, replied: "The greatest lesson life has taught me is that people who set their mind and heart upon riches are equally disappointed whether they get them or whether they do not."

And Lord Baden-Powell, known the wide world over as the founder of the Boy Scout movement, replied: "The greatest lesson life has taught me is that the only way to true happiness is the way of Jesus Christ, to follow him and to do his will."

A few weeks ago when I read of the Englishman who years ago wrote to several outstanding people and asked them to tell him in a few words about the greatest lesson life had taught them, I decided to write a similar letter to four or five people whom I know and admire—people who have lived long, full, useful lives—and ask them the same question. This I did. Their replies have been received. This morning I want to share them with you. We can all profit from them.

One of the persons to whom I wrote was Dr. Harry Emerson Fosdick. I am sure that almost all of you know who he is. A few of the younger ones present might not know him, but most of you do. Some of you have heard him preach from the great pulpit in Riverside Church. Many of you have heard him over the radio. Others of you have read the books that came from his prolific pen. You know what an influence he has had on the entire religious life of our country. You are familiar with the fact that he was far ahead of his day in his thinking and thus was criticized and condemned by many who misunderstood him. None of this silenced him or caused him to change his course. All this you know. Before I give his reply to my question, let me tell you a bit about him that you might not know.

His father was a schoolteacher in Buffalo, New York. Like schoolteachers today, he was greatly underpaid. So young Harry Emerson Fosdick knew what it was to see his father and mother struggling to make ends meet. But in his home there were things money could not buy. There was culture, love, understanding, and there was religion. When he reached high school he began trying to speak in public, but was so shy and embarrassed he almost gave it up.

The psychologists have a timetable of average ages when the critical faculties of boys and girls wake up and doubt begins. To Harry Emerson Fosdick it came a little late, but it came. During his freshman year in college he went home for vacation and announced as impressively as he could to his parents that he had made up his mind that he believed in evolution. His father replied, "Well, I believed that before you were born."

By the time he reached his sophomore year in college, doubt really set in. His childish answers and concepts were not enough, so he dropped them and began struggling for better answers.

When he left home for college at the beginning of his junior year he said to his mother: "I'll behave as though there were a God, but mentally I'm going to clear God out of the universe and start all over to see what I can find."[1]

With that bit of background, let me read you the reply he wrote to my letter last week. Here it is:

> Now in my eighty-fifth year, life has taught me so many lessons that I hesitate to call any one the greatest. But one central and basic lesson is clear: the absolute necessity of faith in God if human life is to have any ultimate meaning. Without God, matter is the creator and we are the chance products of the collision of protons and neutrons, etc. We can put our purposes and meanings into life, but when the earth—and any other planet—once uninhabitable becomes uninhabitable again, all is over. Everything will be as though nothing had ever been before.
>
> With faith in God, however, all that is changed. We have mind behind the universe, purpose running through it, destiny ahead of it. Human life is no longer ultimately meaningless but eternally meaningful. In that faith even death becomes victory.

What a contrast between that statement and the one he made to his mother when he was a junior in college! He made the long journey from doubt to mature faith. And what a faith he has! History will probably record him as the greatest preacher America has yet produced.

I have been told that while he was at his peak as a preacher at Riverside Church in New York, a man whose faith had been shaken and almost destroyed by a series of tragedies went to see him. When the man came out of Dr. Fosdick's study that day, he said to a church secretary, "What a man! When I went in there all the stars had fallen out of my sky, and he put them back one by one."

How many people Dr. Fosdick has led from doubt to a mature faith we shall never know. The number must be tremendous.

Now let us swing from one of the greatest preachers of our land to a humble layman whose life has been touched with greatness. Let us swing from one in New York whom some of you have never seen to one who has often worshipped here with us.

Among the letters I wrote, I addressed one of them to our good friend, Samuel Bell Williams, who is now ninety years of age. Most of you know his life's story, so I shall just touch upon it. Seventy-one years ago he left his home in Tennessee and went to California to grow up with the country. There as he rode the range he came in contact with an occasional Indian. He was a young man, unmarried then but already deeply religious. Consequently he shared his faith with the Indians and converted many of them and started a church for them. Later, married and living on his own ranch, he organized a church and was its leading member. Still later when he moved to Fresno where his children could seek an education, he became a leader in his church and community. His exploits are well known all over the great San Joaquin Valley. His life's story is almost a legend.

Today you cannot be with him five minutes without becoming aware of his deep and sincere Christian faith. He is a remarkable man, an unforgettable character. His mind seems to have a built-in paintbrush that colors everything with lavish, thrilling colors. He is able to see beauty in unexpected places and finds the footprints of God everywhere.

I wrote to him and asked him what was the greatest lesson life had taught him. In his reply he begins by saying that he had just come in from the garden and found my second letter prodding him to write. Then he goes on to write:

I must say I have had a long and happy life. Today at more than ninety years of age the sunlight of heaven still shines beautifully upon the pathway of my life. Life's greatest lesson came to me when I accepted Jesus Christ at the age of thirteen. He has been so real to me that I feel I write these words in his presence.

I once heard of a little boy who in the expression work of a Sunday school class tried to draw a picture of the stilling of the tempest. He drew splendid waves, a fine boat, great angry clouds, and frightened men huddled in the boat. "You haven't drawn Jesus," said his teacher. "No," said the boy quietly, "I couldn't make him beautiful enough."

I think of that story whenever I hear Sam Williams speak about Christ. Although he has great descriptive powers and uses colorful language, I have the feeling that when he tries to paint the picture of Christ in words and tell how much he means to him, Sam can't make him beautiful enough, tremendous enough, significant enough, appealing enough, satisfying enough.

At the age of thirteen he fell in love with Christ, and from that loving relationship has come the greatest lesson of his life.

Now let us switch over to another. Let us swing this time from one most of you have seen worshipping here at times with us to one few if any of you have ever seen. Let us swing clear across the Atlantic Ocean to London and listen to what Leslie D. Weatherhead has to say.

Leslie Weatherhead was born in London in 1893; that makes him seventy. He was educated at Richmond Theological College, London University, and Manchester University. He spent several years in India, and later served Methodist churches in Manchester and Leeds. Then in 1936 he was called to City Temple in London, where he stayed until 1961 when he retired. What Riverside Church is to New York, City Temple is to London—though it is not as beautiful. Leslie Weatherhead, one of the great pulpit voices of Christendom, has inspired thousands upon thousands from all over the world with his spiritual conviction and faith. His sermons, preached often to crowds of university students pestered by doubts, to scientists and educators with intellectual problems, and to the aged with their fears, have been as welcome as carts loaded with sacks of wheat in a starving day.

I didn't write to Dr. Weatherhead to ask him what was the greatest lesson life had taught him. I didn't have to. In 1961 when I was there, just before he retired, he told the congregation what it was and I jotted it down on an envelope. Said Dr. Weatherhead:

> If after forty-five years in the ministry you were to ask me what lesson I had learned more clearly than any other, I would say without any hesitation that I have learned that life will only work out successfully one way, and that is God's way.

I wish I could get all of our young people together and get them to see this. Young people so often get in with the wrong crowd and are led on and on. If only they would take stock occasionally and ask: Where is this path of action leading me?

Life will only work out successfully one way, my young friends, and that is God's way—the way of honesty and decency and fidelity. I wish I could get each young man in our church who is soon to graduate from college and go out on his own to see this. I wish all the young couples whom it is my privilege to marry could realize this. Life will only work out successfully one way, and that is God's way.

Now let us quickly swing back home again to one this congregation knows well and loves greatly. He was for many years a colleague of several of you. Many of you sat at his feet as students when he was the head of the department of religion at the University of Richmond. He taught many of you much of what you know about the Bible and about God. Twice he has served as interim pastor of this church. All of us have been greatly blessed by this most unusual man. He is like a great and shining light to our city. I am speaking, of course, of Solon Cousins. He had a hard time boiling down what he wanted to say. After writing it out several times and then trying again, he came to my study and explained in eloquent words what he had written. I wish I had the time to share every word of it with you. He may be retired, but his keen mind hasn't bogged down. He continues to keep abreast of truth. To have fellowship with him is a rare privilege and a great blessing.

Here in part is what he writes in answer to my question, "What is the greatest lesson life has taught you?"

> What I am saying wells up out of my harvest of the years and my ever-deepening convictions. Life has taught me that Jesus gives the satisfying answers to the basic question that life puts to us. It

has taught me that prayer is significant, worthwhile, important, necessary. It has taught me that the church is not just another social institution—there is something cosmic, supernatural, eternal, triumphant in its life and struggles. But beside all this, life has taught me—and this is my most precious faith—to be a Christian optimist. Here my favorite Christian poet speaks for me:

"One who never turned his back but marched, breast forward, / Never doubted clouds would break, / Never dreamed, though right were worsted, wrong would triumph, / Held, we fall to rise, are baffled to fight better, / Sleep to wake."[2]

A Christian optimist! Would to God we could all learn to be that. God not only once spoke. He still speaks. He not only once worked; he is still working. He has not folded up. Truth and right may founder, but in the end they will triumph. God will prevail. Has life taught you that yet? It has taught Solon Cousins that, and he is thus able to face the rest of life and even the great beyond in hope and expectancy.

My friends, the purpose of an hour of worship such as this is not to bring people together to shake hands and confirm them in their prejudices, but to bring them into the presence of God. Worship is not for the entertainment of the saints. Worship is for redemptive relationships with Christ.

Out in the world our spiritual appetites are dulled. Here they should be sharpened. Out in the world our hearts grow cold; here they should be warmed. The hour of worship is a quiet little park in the noisy din of our hectic week where we ought to hear God speak. The hour of worship is a little oasis in the desert of our monotonous life where we should be able to satisfy our thirst for things for which our souls cry out.

I trust this has been such an hour for you. As you listened to the words of others, have you not heard God speak through them? Have not your hearts been warmed by their testimonies, your spiritual appetites sharpened? Take these lessons home with you. Feed on them; learn from them. Let not this hour be spent in vain.

Notes

[1] Harry Emerson Fosdick, *For The Living of These Days* (New York: Harper & Brothers, 1956), 54.

[2] Robert Browning, "Epilogue," *Anthology of the World's Best Poems*, vol. 4, selected by Edwin Markham (New York: Wm H. Wise Co., 1950), 2018.

Facing the Days Ahead as a Christian

Revelation 7:1-18

(October 29, 1961)

In October 1844 a shop in Philadelphia displayed the following sign: "This shop is closed in honor of the King of Kings who will appear, about the 22nd of October. Get ready to crown him Lord of all." Many thousands of people, like the shop owner, were thoroughly convinced that Jesus Christ was to return to earth in a physical second coming around October 22 of that year more than a century ago, that this earth would be destroyed by divine action, and that the last judgment would occur afterward.

Many who held to this belief sold their property or gave it away; others left their homes, their jobs, their positions; farmers permitted their crops to go unharvested—all in the fervent expectation that the end of time was at hand. A number of believers made "ascension robes" of white cloth that they planned to wear on this eventful occasion. There were, of course, many others who were quite skeptical and a number who were scoffers who asked: "What if the world should not come to an end?" or "Why should we look forward to such a catastrophe with joy?"

The fateful day arrived. Those who believed that the end of time was at hand met in churches, in homes, on hilltops, and on roofs of houses. Some even assembled in cemeteries so that they might greet the dead as they rose from their graves. The sunset and the night came, and the fervor of the believers was unsurpassed. However, when midnight had come and gone without the appearance of Jesus Christ, the enthusiasm began to wane, and with the dawn the disappointments were almost too grievous to bear. One dear lady kept her "ascension robe" on for a week and then put it off, saying, "The Lord has forgotten us."[1]

Despite the failure of Jesus Christ to appear in Philadelphia, since that year and down to our own times millions of people have fervently believed they would live to see Jesus Christ coming down to earth in clouds of glory, only to be as disappointed as were the believers of 1844. As recently as the spring of 1959, a sizable group from various parts of the country gathered at a farm near Waco, Texas, eagerly awaiting the second coming and the catastrophic end of this world age.

The chief source for the expectation of the immediate second coming of Christ in our time—or any other time—with the destruction of this world age is the book we read our lesson from this morning: the Book of Revelation.

The Book of Revelation has suffered an unfortunate fate. On the whole either it has been abandoned by the readers of the Bible as being almost completely unintelligible, or it has become the happy hunting ground of religious eccentrics who seek to construct from it a kind of celestial timetable of events to come. The obscurity of the Book of Revelation has been felt by scholars in all ages. Jerome complained that the book contained as many riddles as it does words. Luther would have banished it from the pages of the New Testament. Still another scholar said that the Book of Revelation either finds a man mad or leaves him so.

In order for us to understand even a little of what the writer of the Book of Revelation was saying, we have to know something of the background against which he wrote. It is obvious that Revelation was written in a time when Christians were being persecuted by Roman officials for their refusal to worship the emperor. Some Christians who refused to worship the emperor were put to death in horrible ways. Some had skins of animals sewed to their bodies, and then were led into the arena to be torn to pieces by fierce dogs. Others were crucified. Still others had their clothing impregnated with pitch and oil, and then when their garments had been set on fire they became human torches. Much of this took place in Rome in the newly completed coliseum. But Rome wasn't the only place where Christians were persecuted. About the same time Christians were being dragged into the coliseum in Rome, a persecution of Christians broke out in Asia Minor, whose chief city was Ephesus. All of this took place near the end of the first century A.D.

The situation was desperate. How could the Christians continue to remain loyal and faithful in the face of such danger and trial? The future of Christianity was greatly endangered.

It was to meet this pressing danger that John, in exile at Patmos, wrote the Book of Revelation. His main purpose in writing it was to encourage, embolden, and inspire the Christians to live worthily and face the day with faith and courage. He assured the Christians that God had not forgotten them and that right would in the end prevail. He promised them that martyrs would be gloriously rewarded. The sun would never burn them. They would never hunger or thirst. There would be no need to cry again, so there would be no more tears (Rev. 7:15-18).

To get across this message of hope, encouragement, and faith, the writer used symbols—many symbols and weird figures of speech. This is what makes parts of the letter so difficult for us to understand. But this much we do know: The Book of Revelation is not a celestial timetable of events to come. It is not a crystal ball into which we can gaze and predict the future. Its primary purpose was to encourage, embolden, and inspire the early Christian in a trying and terrifying day.

No doubt there are some people today who wish we could use the book as a crystal ball and predict the future. We ask ourselves: Should I build a fallout shelter? Is a nuclear war inevitable? Will the earth and life on it soon be destroyed? What does the day ahead hold for us?

My friends, I can't answer those questions for you. Nor can anyone else. Those who use the Book of Revelation as if it were a crystal ball predicting the future misuse it. God has given us the power to comprehend, to grasp, and to understand the present. Through the use of memory we can look back and see with the mind's eye what took place yesterday. But God has not given us the ability to gaze across tomorrow. Tomorrow lies hidden from us. The future is hidden from us, for one thing, because it is not yet made. The future is not something already created and waiting, as it were, on the other side of a curtain, because God has entrusted to us a part in the making of it.

While I cannot predict what the days ahead hold for us, I would like to try at least to tell you how I believe a Christian should face the trying and uncertain days ahead.

Think for a moment. If someone came and asked you how a person should face the days ahead—in what spirit, in what attitude—what would you say? How would you put it in words? Suppose your child, young in years but old enough to grasp the feel of things, should listen to the news and suddenly realize that terror stalks our world and fear hides behind every door. Suppose that child should say to you, "Daddy, what can we do? What ought we to do? How should we face the days ahead?" Those questions are being asked. They are important questions. How shall we answer them?

I have thought a great deal about this. It's not an easy matter with which to cope. Indeed, I hardly know whether my answer is really worthwhile, but I feel I must say something on this urgent matter.

I have not come here to say to you that you should cease building fallout shelters, and trust God more and things will be all right: We can depend on God too much—in that we can depend on God to do things for us that he will not do. I have said this on many different occasions, but I say it again. God never has done for man that which man can and ought to do for himself, and I don't believe he is going to start now. How then should we face the days ahead?

The first thing I would like to say concerning this is that we should face the days ahead with hope and courage.

That's not easy, you say. I know it isn't. Events of the day tend to dry up our hope and courage like the broiling sun dries up the morning dew. Nothing that is worthwhile is easy—remember that.

So long as we live we must never give up in despair and sit down hopeless and say war is inevitable. Norman Cousins is right: "War becomes inevitable if we believe it to be inevitable. We can talk our way into race suicide. Once the idea of inevitability is accepted by one side or the other, it is only a matter of time before the nuclear fire-storm begins." As Christians we must never believe in the inevitability of war. We must be physically prepared for it but never give up hope that it can be avoided. Once we become hopeless we cease trying to find ways to be understanding.

I am still hopeful because our leaders are still trying to find ways to peace. I am hopeful because I am aware that the leaders of the world know all too well that in a nuclear war there will be no winner—but mutual suicide. Fear of mutual suicide may yet force man to live with his neighbor. Behind our schools is the fear of illiteracy and ignorance. Behind our medical science is the fear of dread disease. From lighthouses on perilous seacoasts to democracy trying to displace crushing tyranny, man's positive response to danger has been one of the most creative factors in his experience. Ralph Waldo Emerson once said, "Fear is an instructor of great sagacity and the herald of all revolutions."

God grant that fear may have that consequence now in preventing a nuclear war! Personally, I am hopeful that it will.

I cannot avoid taking courage from still another source: the unexpected, unforeseeable victories of right over wrong in history. Victor Hugo was once trying to explain the defeat and ruin of Napoleon and he said, "Napoleon fell into ruin because he bothered God." Just a few years ago Hitler seemed to be on top of the world. Did Hitler last? On the contrary, who ever fell more ignominiously from the peak of success into the abyss of defeat and shame? Of course that doesn't prove that Russia will not push us into war, or that some accidental mistake may not trigger an explosion of insane nuclear slaughter. But I cannot read history without feeling hopeful in my bones.

Face the days ahead, then, with hope and courage. That's first.

Second, we should face the days ahead with the determination to do all we can to keep the moral level of our society high.

This becomes doubly important because it is possible for a nation to collapse from within.

Have you ever visited Trinity Church in Boston? There used to be a bay where Trinity Church now stands. The bay was filled in and, thus all around Trinity Church the land is manmade and the water is only a few feet under the sidewalk. Trinity Church was built in 1877 and rests on 4,500 wooden piles. You know as well as I do that wood does not rot so long as it is kept in water. Let the water level drop and air get to the piles, and that is the end of the wood. Thus, Trinity church has a committee in charge of water levels. The committee is responsible for seeing that the water is kept at a level high enough to protect the piles and keep them from rotting.

Wouldn't this make a good parable? If the level of our moral and spiritual life falls too low, the foundations of our society will begin to crumble. We can fall by decaying from within. All of us must think of ourselves as members of a committee to protect the moral water levels of our society.

I talked recently with a woman in great trouble. She said to me: "My family hasn't been near a church for a long time. We haven't paid anything on our pledge for two years. We have been living like pigs, and that sort of life is tearing the hell out of my soul. We must straighten out and live right." Are you and your family adding your bucketful to the moral water levels of our society? This woman admitted that she and her family were failing to do this.

We should face the days ahead with the determination to do all we can to keep the moral level of our society high. That's second.

Third, instead of facing the days ahead crying, "Who will show us any good?" we should face the days ahead saying, "It's a trying time, I know, but still a great time and I am glad to be alive and have some small part in it."

During the darkest days of the last war I saved up a little money and went to New York City to spend a weekend. When Sunday morning came I went over to Riverside Church to hear Dr. Harry Emerson Fosdick preach. I had never before been to New York, nor had I ever heard Dr. Fosdick in person. When I arrived at Riverside Church, I gazed at the bulletin board and saw the sermon subject for the morning. What do you think it was? He was preaching that morning on the subject, "A Great Time to Be Alive." I have never forgotten that sermon. It made a lasting impression on me. He began by saying, "This certainly is a ghastly time to be alive." He went on to point out that behind the stirring headlines that narrate the clash of armies an unheralded mass of human misery existed, the like of which our earth had seldom, if ever, seen before. Then he rose to his full height as a preacher and cried out, "It is a ghastly time to be alive. But that is only half of it. It is also a great time to be alive." Why did he think it was a great time to be alive? Because, he said, history was pushing us out of our ruts and saying now you have got to change, men were being driven back to the fundamentals; they were being caught up in a great revolution that demanded their best. Such a time, he said, is a great time in which to be alive.

Cannot this be said of our day? It is a trying time, yes. Terror stalks our world. Fear creeps into our homes, our lives, and even our dreams. But it is also a great time to be alive. New frontiers are opening as men soar out into space. Nuclear power can be put to noble purposes. Breakthroughs in medical science will soon take place. Men, I believe, will soon be pushed away from their desire to seek nothing but pleasure and a good time and come back to the fundamentals. Religious leaders—preachers, if you will—will, I believe, be compelled to cease talking about nonsense and dig deeper into God's truth and come up with a more intelligent understanding of our Christian faith. It's a ghastly time, I admit, but it is also a great time to be alive—and don't you forget it.

Build your fallout shelter if you wish and if you can. There is nothing wrong with that. But then don't go and sit down shrouded with pessimism and spend your time weeping and wringing your hands. Face tomorrow with hope and courage. Make your contribution to the moral water level of our society. And be glad that you are alive in such a revolutionary time when each life can count for so much.

One man told me recently: "I do not know what the days ahead may bring, but I plan to live as nobly as I can and do my uttermost for my church, my country, and my God. If I have to go out, I want to go out with a bang and not a whimper." Can we do any better?

Note

[1] This story came from Martin Rist, *The Modern Reader's Guide to the Book of Revelation* (New York: Association Press, 1961).

To Which Church Would Jesus Belong?

Hebrews 12:2

(November 1956)

A question raised by Harold Cooke Phillips of Cleveland, Ohio, intrigues me a great deal. "To which church," he asks, "would Jesus belong today?" Now that, in my opinion, is not a facetious question. Rather, it is a sober inquiry that needs to be given serious thought. For the church that would meet the Master's approval is the type most needed in our world today and the one that should interest us, isn't it? How shall we approach this matter if our answer to the question is to be fair and worthwhile?

According to the *Yearbook of American Churches* for 1956, there are 300,056 churches in this country. And, of course, there are thousands and thousands in other countries. To which of these churches would Jesus belong? To say that Jesus would belong to one of these and not the others would be no more than a wild guess. Who knows the heart and soul of all those congregations? So, I would close that avenue of approach.

A second avenue of approach would be to look at the different religious bodies or denominations. There are 268 religious bodies or denominations in this country. Think of it—268. Of that number, 256 are Protestant. To be sure, many of them are only splinter groups, for 25 percent of American Protestants are in only 14 denominations. The fact remains, however, that all told there are 256 Protestant denominations. Then there are the Catholics, Eastern Orthodox, Christian Science, and a few others—268 in all. To which of these churches would Jesus belong? Some people following their own prejudices would, no doubt, without any hesitation suggest their own denomination, whatever that may be. But frankly I haven't the audacity to venture a guess. I should like, though, to suggest still another and a better avenue of approach to the question. To approach it along denominational lines is dangerous and divisive.

Dr. Henry Pitney Van Dusen, president of Union Theological Seminary in New York City, has said that generally and broadly speaking there are only three types of Christian churches or three great divisions, and that these divisions stretch across all denominations. In other words, he is saying, it seems to me, there are three large categories and all our churches regardless of denomination can be placed in one of the three. Now, if that is true—and I believe it is—we can look at the characteristics of these three types of churches and come to some conclusion as which type of church best measures up to the spirit and teaching of Jesus. This method of approach would not be unfair or divisive.

First of all, there is the "reactionary church." The reactionaries have many good qualities. They are sincere. They are loyal to the church. They are people of personal integrity. They have convictions. But in spite of all these good and admirable traits, they are usually quite hard to get along with. Moreover, as the history of church abundantly shows, they can cause a lot of trouble and do a considerable amount of harm. Some of the darkest pages of church history—such as the Inquisition when people were hunted down, tortured, and martyred—were written by the reactionaries.

The reactionaries are those who believe not only that they have the truth, but also that they possess all the truth there is. They are not satisfied with a ray of light from the sun; they think they own the sun. Hence the reactionaries are quite narrow in their outlook, and at times are overbearingly arrogant. They reveal what John Wesley referred to as "that miserable big try which makes many so unready to believe that there is any work of God but among themselves." Moreover, they regard truth as something finished and static. God has spoken but no longer speaks. The God they worship shows his glory in the western sky. They do not look eastward to see him in the light of dawn. Such, in brief, and one hopes not too unfairly, is the reactionary church. And there are reactionary churches in every major denomination.

The second category under which many churches would come is the "conventional church." If you turn to Webster's dictionary and look up the word conventional, this is what you would find: "Growing out of, or depending on custom, established or sanctioned by general concurrence or usage. Hence, lacking spontaneity, originality, or individuality; ordinary; or trite." Let us leave Webster now and try to describe the conventional church in our own words. It has, at least, three characteristics.

The conventional church is made up of people who never expect anything out of the ordinary to happen. They do not think, as do the reactionaries, that God no longer speaks. But they seem to think that God is not saying anything important, and that it does not make much difference whether they listen or not.

Again, the conventional Christians are those who never take their religion very seriously. They will contribute, attend, or serve when they feel like it or when it suits their convenience. They are not arrogant like the reactionary because they do not believe profoundly enough to have any deep convictions.

Then, too, the conventional Christians are usually staunch defenders of the status quo. They accept the comfort and consolation of Christianity, but avoid its challenge and discipline. Such, in brief, is the conventional church. And there are churches of that kind in every denomination.

There is still a third category or kind of church: the "creative church." The creative churches are the courageous churches. They are courageous because of unbounded faith in God. They are not afraid of new truth—provided, mind you, that it is truth. When some new theory is advanced in the field of science, psychology, or something else that seems to contradict or change some traditional religious belief, they are not unduly alarmed. They argue that if this new idea is really true, it must be God's truth—for God is the source of all truth and cannot be divided against himself.

And so, when Copernicus or Galileo or Darwin or someone else advances some new theory of the universe or human life, the creative church does not, first of all, begin to fight them; rather, it begins to listen to them, to try to understand them. It tries to distinguish between the essential and the incidental, the picture and the frame, the scaffolding and the building, the treasure and the earthen vessel.

The creative church is also the pioneering church. It leads the way into new fields of service, seeks new methods, blazes new trails. It seeks to bring religion down from the clouds where some are wont to put it and apply it to the various problems of day-by-day living. The creative church is the church that responds to the leading of the Holy Spirit. It is spiritually awake and alive. And there are churches here and there from many denominations that come in this category.

Perhaps at this point it would help to pull our thoughts together if we used a comparison. The Christian church has been likened to a ship. The anchor represented the reactionaries. Anchors are necessary, yet a ship that perpetually lies at anchor is hardly true to its nature.

The largest part of the ship, the hull, symbolizes the conventional church. It is not at anchor, yet seems to lack both direction and power. It yields, conforms easily to the passing pressure of wind and wave. It follows uncritically the tides of opinion and custom.

The creative church is likened to the sails spread to catch the winds of God, and moving in the direction of his purpose. It responds to the leading of the Holy Spirit.

Now to which of these churches would Jesus belong?

Surely we would not find him among the reactionaries. The reactionaries were the ones who opposed him most bitterly and played so large a role in his crucifixion. He chided the reactionaries of his day for their failure to distinguish between the essentials and non-essentials of religion. The reactionaries are the nursemaids of superstition and bigotry, the enemy of science and truth. Surely we would not find the master and pioneer of our faith there.

Nor would he be found in the conventional church, among those for whom religion is an outward form, lacking in inner power. He would not feel at home among the lovers of the status quo. He was too adventuresome for that.

No! There is no doubt that Christ would feel more at home in the creative church.

Is our church a creative church?

That is a question we should ask ourselves over and over again as the years come and go. Is our church one that the fearless, adventuresome, pioneering Christ would feel at home in? Are we spiritually awake and alive, responding to the leading of the Holy Spirit? Are we courageous enough to move out and blaze new trails if need be in spite of the criticism that may come? Do we believe not only that God has spoken, but also that he still speaks? Have we been trying to take religion and apply it to life as it must be lived today? Do we have unbounded faith in God?

On the first Sunday in November 1950—six full years ago—I stood up in the large room that is now the administrative wing and tried to preach my first sermon as pastor of this new church. How the time has sped by! About the only way I can realize that I have been here six full years is to look back at your long line of accomplishments, to observe how many of our young people have grown into young manhood and womanhood, or to glance in the mirror at the gray hairs that have taken up their abode on my head. They have not been easy years for me, but they have been happy ones. To have the opportunity to work with this new and growing church and to be the pastor of some of the finest people I have ever known is an experience for which I shall ever be grateful. All during the past six years, one of the dreams that has claimed my life was to try and lead this church to be a creative one. The goal may not have been reached as yet. But I am bold enough to say that I believe we are on the way and on the right track. This morning at this sacred table of our Lord I shall dedicate myself anew to the complete fulfillment of that dream, and I ask that you do the same.

The hope of the Christian cause as it faces the future lies in the creative church, a church that is courageous because it trusts God; adventurous because it follows one who is on the march and goes before us—the Pioneer of Faith; one that works for cooperation and unity among Christians and thus seeks to help make Christ's prayer "that they may all be one" a reality. To be a member of the creative church is to join the church to which Christ belongs.

What Should You Tell a Child about God?

Genesis 7:1-24

(February 18, 1962)

Do you find it difficult to talk to your child about God? Many theologians believe that it's as hard for parents today to tell their children about God as it was for the parents of yesterday to tell them about sex. Is that true? Do you find it difficult to talk to your child about God? If so, why? Is it because the subject is so personal that you bare your soul when you talk about it? Is it because the subject is profound and you find it difficult to talk to your child in language he can understand? Are you afraid that if you are caught talking naturally and normally about God, someone will think you are a bit queer, a square, or a sissy? Or is it difficult for you to talk about God because you feel that you don't know enough about the subject to talk about it intelligently?

One day last week a man, whom I have known and considered a friend for several years but is not a member of this church, bumped into me in a drugstore and while we talked he asked me a question. He wanted to know something about the *Christian Century* magazine and the *InterChurch News*. I told him that the *Christian Century* magazine was one of the most respected religious publications in the country and that the *InterChurch News* was a publication of the World Council of Churches. Then I told him that I subscribed to both publications. Apparently he was surprised, and he asked me why I read them. I told him I wanted to know what was going on in the field of religion outside the Richmond Baptist Association and outside the Southern Baptist Convention. I wanted to try to keep abreast of what was going on in the field of religion all over the world. Then he said that he had seen these publications, and that most of the editorials were about politics, business, and the international situation. These are fields, he said, into which religion ought never to go. Then he made this revealing statement: "Religion has to do with one's emotions—the health of one's emotions—and nothing else."

Now, that is one of the poorest conceptions of what religion is all about that I have ever heard. Religion does have something to do with the health of man's emotions, but to confine it to that is like confining religion to one room in the home or to one hour of the week. Religion must permeate the entire home, all of the hours in the week. It has something to do with all of life—the way we think, act, play, and run our business—the way we live every hour of every day.

I have wondered about my friend several times since our conversation. If his conception of God is as inadequate as his conception of religion, I wonder how he would be able to ever talk to a child about God.

Is a lack of knowledge about God one of the things that makes it difficult for you to talk to your child about God? What should we tell a child about God?

Back in the December issue of *Redbook* magazine there appeared an article titled, "What You Should Not Tell a Child about God." An abbreviated version of it appears in this month's *Reader's Digest*. It was a very good article, and I hope you have read it. This morning I want to think with you about what we should tell a child about God. It is a difficult subject, but an important one. How shall we begin?

Let's begin by asking: What should we tell a child about how God created the world?

In the article that appeared in *Redbook*, the writer states that if we foolishly allow our children to think that religion accounts for the creation of the world in one way and science in another, a time may come when they will leave their faith behind along with their trains and dolls in the cupboards of childhood.

What, then, should we tell our children about how God created the world? I dealt with this matter in detail a year or so ago; therefore I shall not go into great detail with this question this morning. I will, in just a few simple lines, tell you how I think you should talk about this problem to a child.

You should point out to the child that there are many stories in the literature of the world that tell how man has thought God created the world. Two of these stories that differ widely are in our Bible. One is in the first chapter of Genesis, and the other one is in the second and third chapters of Genesis. Then I would point out that scientists of today have their theories as to how God did it. Then I would try to make it clear that the two beautiful stories of creation found in our Bible represent the very best thought of ancient man. We do not know whether everything happened exactly the way they said or not, because nobody was there but God. But even if the world did not begin exactly as these old stories say it began, we can be sure of two things.

The first is that it was God who created the world. It was he who brought order out of chaos. Just exactly how he did it we will never know. But we believe that it was God who did it, and in his own mysterious and wonderful way.

The second thing we can be sure of is that this great God who created the world is the same God who brought man into existence. It may have taken him, as our scientists now believe, millions of years to do it instead of a day as the story in Genesis states, but it was God who did it. He created us because he loved us. He has never stopped loving us. And he will keep on loving us forever.

What should we tell our children about God and the matter of punishment?

The writer of the article in *Redbook* goes on to say that we should not tell a child that God is watching him to see whether he is good. This, the writer states, leads a child to think of God as someone who keeps an eye on him and that he might smack him down if he should ever disobey. This, says the writer, is a concept too grievous for him. He is too small, and God is too big. If you have read the article to which I have made reference, then perhaps you recall this story.

A seven-year-old boy was building a model plane and was so intent that he reached up to the shelf for a pair of scissors without looking and quite by accident broke a treasured Havilland plate. He burst into tears. "It was your best plate," he wailed. "But you didn't mean to," his mother soothed him. "We don't punish little boys for things like that." "God does," said the little fellow. "All those people in the world when the flood came . . . Do you think they all meant to be bad? But he drowned them, every one."

Let me draw aside just a moment to say a few words about the flood story and Noah and his ark—the story the little lad was referring to.

There is ample evidence that the people in the Tigris-Euphrates Valley were visited by a terrible flood in the days when ancestors of the early Hebrews lived there. Recent excavations at several sites provide evidence of such a flood that struck a city with such devastating force that twenty-five feet of debris settled in one place before it was overlaid by nine feet of river-washed sand and silt. Scholars estimate that the flood must have been of such violence as to sweep the entire valley clean of all life that had not found its way to the mountains far to the west. And, of course, since the floodwaters came tumbling from the mountains, they were thought to be evidence of the wrath of God over the wickedness of men. This occurred one thousand years before the days of Abraham, or about 2,700 B.C. It was around this happening in the Tigris-Euphrates Valley that the story of the flood and Noah and his ark grew up.

Today, after great rains when people in low-lying regions are flooded, we no longer think of it as the wrath of God smacking down helpless people who have disobeyed him. We sell bond issues and put in flood control measures and improved drainage facilities. But not so in the long, long ago when the race of man was young. They thought a flood was sent by an angry God to punish them.

Now let me get back to our question. What shall we today tell a child about God and the matter of punishment?

Say this to your child: God loves you very much, just as your father and mother love you. God wants you to grow up and be a very fine person, He knows that growing up takes a long time and that sometimes it is a rather painful process. He understands that when you are very young, it is often difficult to get along with some people. He realizes that it takes a lot of practice and a great deal of living to love people all of the time. God does not want you to keep on making mistakes, but he knows that you will make a good many of them in your life and that you will probably never grow old enough, or wise enough, to keep from making some. All of us make mistakes, even when we are grown. But we keep trying to make fewer of them, and we try most of all to learn lessons from them.

When you make a mistake or do something wrong, God expects you to say that you are sorry and that you will try not to make the mistake again. He will forgive you and love you as if you never did anything wrong, even though he knows that you did. For, you see, God is not interested in remembering the wrong things you have done. He wants, most of all, for you to be a very fine person. It will take courage to admit your mistakes, faults, and shortcomings and ask God to forgive you. But when you do this, you will discover something very wonderful. You will find out God is not waiting to punish you, slap you down, scold you, or make you miserable, but that he has been waiting all the time for you to ask for forgiveness that he might give it to you and enable you to go on toward becoming a much better person.

Is this not what we should tell a child? God is not an over-indulgent grandfather who sees nothing wrong in us. I'm not saying that. He is a loving understanding Father who will forgive us, if we seek forgiveness, and help us to go on and become our best.

Come with me a little further now as we ask: What should we tell a child about God's willingness to answer prayer?

Should we tell him that all he has to do is to pray earnestly for anything he wants and presto, he will get it? If we do, we are making a grave mistake.

Do you remember how Philip Corey in Somerset Maugham's *Of Human Bondage* prayed passionately and believingly every night that God would take away his clubfoot? How eagerly he waited for the morning of the day when he had asked God to make it come true. What plans he had made for that day. At breakfast time he would run down the stairs, three steps at a time, and everyone would be so surprised; then he would go buy a new pair of shoes, and at school that very day he would play football. The morning came. Joyously he reached under the bedclothes to touch the new foot, but there was the old one, just as before, ugly and deformed as ever.

A child's faith can be like that, as big as the world and as unquestioning. What should we tell a child concerning God and the matter of prayer?

Before I try to put this into words such as you might use when talking to a child, let me remind you of a few things concerning the matter of praying. We must remember that prayer is not a magic wand by which a person can get everything he may ask for. If so, then we would be the rulers of the universe and not God. We must remember that just because we are good is no guarantee that God will look upon us as his favorites.

During the Great Plague in England in 1665, many Christian people must have prayed to God, "Lord, save my husband; save my child; save my lover from the plague!" But if God, in response to prayer, had had favorites, do you realize that plague would still be with us? Men would have thought that the way to treat plague was to pray.

When Jesus called Peter, he did not say to him: "Peter, follow me! Your fishing business will always prosper. You and your family will be immune from disease." God has no favorites. Then, too, we need to remember that prayer should not be used to get God to do for us the things we should do for ourselves. Finally, remember that even though we offer a worthy and answerable prayer in the spirit of Jesus Christ, God still uses his own judgments in giving an answer.

With this in mind, then, say to your child: God wants you to share your hopes, dreams, and desires with him through prayer. God wants you to tell him about everything, just as your mother and father want you to tell them about your problems. I am sure that God listens to every prayer and that he wants to do every good thing for you that he can. But he leaves many things up to you, because you could not grow up to be a man or a lady if he did everything for you. You should pray to God often to thank him for what he has given you. But you should not ask God to do for you what you should do for yourself. If you want to get better marks in school, you must study harder. God will not spoil you by giving you good marks just because you pray to him. If you want a bicycle, you should not expect God to give you one. Ask your parents, or better still, earn the money yourself by selling papers, mowing lawns, or shoveling snow. God is not a Santa Claus who gives you whatever you ask for. He is a loving father who gives you many gifts, but who also expects you to do for yourself what can be done only by you.

Now, perhaps we come to the hardest question of all: What should we tell a child about God's relation to the matter of death?

This is no light matter, for death thrusts a sharp sword into our hearts. Human ties that have meant so much for so many years are suddenly and finally severed. It is as if a deep-rooted plant were pulled out of the heart with a tearing and wounding of the heart.

Sometimes we may say to a child that God took the one who died. This I think is wrong. It leads the child to think of God as someone who steals from him what he loves most. God takes a person only after death releases him. Sometimes we may tell a child that the person has gone away. This, I feel, is inadequate, for the child will look for his return and be disappointed.

If grandmother dies and the child should ask where grandmother has gone, what has happened to her, perhaps this is what we should say: Grandma lived a long time and was getting quite old. She was sick, and finally her body died. Her body was no longer strong enough and well enough for her to use it. So when this happens, God lets our bodies die. Then, the best in us, which some call our spirits and others call our personality and still others call our soul, must live somewhere else. The Bible teaches that this best side of us goes to heaven and lives in another kind of body called a spiritual body.

We don't know where heaven is, but we know that it is where God is. If we don't learn about life and about God while we live on earth, we shall probably have to start in the lower grades in the school of heaven. But the important thing to remember is that when the body grows too sick or too old to be of use, it dies and is buried in the ground, but we live in new spiritual bodies with God forever—where nothing can separate us from his love.

What should we tell a child about God? It's not an easy question to answer. To do it, you bare your own soul. But we must try as best we can. And as we try, who knows but that God will become more real to us?

Vernon Britt Richardson
(Pastor, 1964-1970)

Vernon Britt Richardson, a native of Portsmouth, Virginia, was born on May 19, 1914, the son of Norwood B. Richardson and Lillian Bell Britt, and was reared in a warm Christian environment that greatly influenced his formative years. Dr. Richardson entered the University of Richmond in 1931 and graduated with a B.A. While a student at the university he was the associate editor of the campus newspaper; president of the junior class; president of the social fraternity Phi Epsilon; manager of the baseball team; a cheerleader; and a member of the national leadership fraternity *Omicron Delta Kappa*, national journalism fraternity *Pi Delta Epsilon*, and national debating fraternity *Tau Kappa Alpha*. He earned the B.D. degree from Crozer Theological Seminary in Pennsylvania, and did additional graduate studies at the University of Pennsylvania and served two years in a fellowship at Cambridge University in England.

He received an honorary Doctor of Divinity degree from his alma mater, the University of Richmond, in 1949. Later he would be called by Dr. George Modlin, president of the University of Richmond, as "one of the University of Richmond's most distinguished alumni." He served the university as vice rector and as a member of the executive committee of the board of trustees.

When Richardson returned to the United States from his studies in England, he began his first pastorate at Westhampton Baptist Church in Richmond, Virginia, where he served from 1940-1943. In 1939 he was ordained to the ministry. In 1943 he joined the Navy and became a chaplain and served his country for the next three years. During his naval career, Dr. Richardson was awarded four campaign ribbons and four battle stars. He was on the first Allied ship that entered Tokyo Bay at the end of World War II and witnessed the surrender of the Japanese naval forces.

His sweetheart, Francis Martin, from Richmond, Virginia, joined him at Pearl Harbor, Hawaii, where he was stationed as an assistant to the fleet chaplain in the Pacific Theater of War, and they got married there in the summer of 1944. Later they had two children, a daughter Frances Martin, and a son Vernon Britt Richardson, Jr.

In 1946 the elder Richardson became pastor of University Baptist Church in Baltimore, Maryland, near Johns Hopkins University, and served the church for eighteen years until he accepted the call to come to River Road Church in 1964.

In addition to his service as a trustee at the University of Richmond, Dr. Richardson was a member of the Midwestern Baptist Theological Seminary board of trustees, the executive committee of the Baptist World Alliance, the University of Shanghai board of founders, the Southern Baptist Foreign Mission Board, the Maryland Bible Society board of managers, the executive committee of the Maryland Adult Education, and the board of trustees of Crozer Theological Seminary, and an alumnus member of Phi Beta Kappa national scholarship fraternity by the Epsilon Chapter of Virginia.

Upon accepting the call to serve as River Road's pastor in 1964, Dr. Richardson led the church in completing the new sanctuary consecrated in 1969, reaching new members and increasing the congregation to almost 1,400 by 1970, establishing a closer working relationship with the

University of Richmond, and offering new ministries to college students and others.

In December 1970, Dr. Richardson experienced chest and abdominal pains and was admitted to the Medical College of Virginia for a gall bladder disorder. He underwent surgery but the infection had spread to other organs, and he became worse and died two days after his surgery on December 6, 1970, at the age of 56. Although Dr. Richardson's pastorate lasted only six years, his vision left an indomitable impact on the future life of the congregation.

My Dream for This Church

Genesis 37:19

(May 2, 1965)

The brothers of Joseph meant it in ridicule when they said of him, "Behold this dreamer cometh." They went on to add, "Let us slay him and then see what will become of his dreams."

Your minister frankly admits to being a dreamer, but it is devoutly to be wished that his dreams not provoke that same reaction on the part of his brethren here at River Road Church! It is a pastor's duty to dream and, as Lowell said of poets, "listening to the inner flow of things, speak to the age out of eternity."

In the case of Joseph, the dreams were literal: visualizations during slumber. Today we use the term to describe visualizations while very much awake, letting the mind range down the years to look upon what can be. In that sense, I would hope that every one of us, so far as the church is concerned, would have it said of him: "Behold, this dreamer cometh."

Every great human achievement has existed first within the mind of a dreamer. Dreams are the inner flame that gives light and inspiration to mankind to do what he must—and what he may. John A. Broadus dreamed of a seminary for a trained ministry in the South, and in 1865, amid the rubble left by war, said to his three colleagues on the faculty: "Let us agree that the Seminary may die, but that we will die first." Today the Southern Baptist Theological Seminary of Louisville is one of the greatest in the world and one of the largest.

I have dreams for this church. I hope you have, too. I came here, responding to your call, because I believe I share a dream with you. For one thing, I see in my mind's eye a church here on this high and holy place that will have the spiritual simplicity and enthusiasm of the churches of the New Testament. Those two qualities go together, for one can never generate enthusiasm for a confusion or an ambivalence or a vague generality. The churches of the New Testament were communities of faith centered on the person of Jesus as the visible expression of God, and, therefore, the Lord of life. Cried Peter to the authorities, "That one whom you slew God exalted." They were certain of that! There could be glorious disarray and uncertainty over many things in the early Christian church, but of Christ they were sure. It was the source of their enthusiasm and their single-mindedness—another word for simplicity. They were in the world to serve Christ and to grow unto his likeness. I dream of that in this church.

No matter how large we may become, however influential, this is primary. The men and women of the New Testament churches found a glory in life. "The weary weight of an unintelligible world" had settled upon the Greeks and Romans; their gods could no longer support them. Then the heavens opened; a new meaning was given to life, new revelation, new glory, and it was a glory that shone in the face of Jesus Christ!

Our world needs this lift of restored meaning to lead it out of desperation into enthusiasm and zest for living. When one looks back to the early church, the quality he wishes most for us to possess is the sense that life is worth the best we can bring to it, even if that best be our dying.

Moreover, let us dream of a church that has in it the grandeur and mystery of the churches of the Middle Ages. When one visits the great churches of Europe today, built in the fourteenth and fifteenth centuries, so often languishing now in spiritual inertia, the smell of death upon them, he cannot escape the feeling as his soul soars to the Gothic heights that some lost grandeur must have existed once to conceive of this and laboriously and sacrificially to have built it.

At Cambridge University I worshipped for two years in King's College Chapel, a place of surpassing beauty. I always pondered the fact that it was finished, standing there in all its strength, when Columbus discovered America in 1492. The contrast in imagery was strong between England's storied past and our savage shores 500 years ago. But greater still, to aid my worship, was the link with the centuries, and with the company of the faithful.

> O where are kings and empires now
> Of old that went and came?
> But, Lord, Thy Church is praying yet,

A thousand years the same.
We mark her goodly battlements,
And her foundations strong:
We hear within the solemn voice of her unending song.[1]

When we come to build our house to God, may we have a sense of history, and build for the ages. In some way, all the ingenuity of craftsmanship, all the skills of engineers, all the artistry of architects must be in service to the soul in its aspiration for that which is beyond us, beyond our tools and toil. The mystery of true worship must linger, rising to fill the temple like smoke from the ancient altars of Israel. Our church must reflect our non-mastery of life.

And let us not be ashamed of beauty. Who can behold a springtime like this one we now know and claim that God prefers the shabby and the mediocre, the ugly and the plain. The Bible says, "He hath made all things beautiful in their time."

I dream of a sanctuary rising here that will be the most beautiful we have ever seen, so that to cross the threshold will be to move the spirit upward. I say this not because I believe as the Greeks did, in the holiness of beauty. Rather, with the ancient Hebrew, I believe in the beauty of holiness. We will not worship the beauty; we will worship in beauty. Sometime, perhaps 500 years from now, if the world lasts that long, some student from the University will worship here and ponder the sacrifice, the vision, the high ventures of the soul that brought this house of God into being, and as his spirit stirs within him, will say with the psalmist of old: "Strength and beauty are in thy sanctuary."

Finally, I dream of a church that will be a full-time instrument in the hand of God, doing his work in the modern world. What businessman would invest millions in property and operate it only four or five hours a week? That is poor business in anybody's eyes; it is certainly so in God's eyes.

Full time will mean seven days a week from eight in the morning until ten o' clock at night, a staff of sextons rotating to meet the material needs. Something helpful will be going on all the time; it will be a veritable university of Christian life where one may elect a field of service and of study. There will be creative opportunities at all levels: family life institutes; workshops in Christian drama, in teacher training, in Biblical studies; community projects for those with special abilities, retired persons, for example. Who can look to the future and not take into account the lengthening of life? The church must help mobilize the talents and redeem the time for those in the later years. "When life's half done, you must give quality to the other half, else you lose both, lose all."

Again our church will provide for those with special needs, the physically handicapped, and the mentally retarded who have an aptitude for learning that God loves them.

Here we will have a daily kindergarten not merely to compete with the public school, but to recognize the importance of those best years for achieving the awareness of God. Impressions of childhood are lasting. Those first years should be filled with the lively sense of a wonderful world with God in it.

Specialized courses for all ages are needed to meet specific needs for the different roles we are to play—as parents, young people, businessmen, educators, homemakers. How else can we become informed, contemporary Christians? Wherever we touch life it should be the touch of Christ, healing, enlightening, redeeming. That is the church's task. It will call for boldness, imagination; creative walk in untrod paths. I believe you are capable of it. I believe God calls us to it.

As for our connection with the University of Richmond, our nearest neighbor, there are unlimited possibilities as it brings the world to our door, with its hundreds of students from this country and abroad, some of them having their first acquaintance with Christianity. Our ministry to students ever beckons, and we have barely begun to do what we can. The late John R. Mott once said, "If I had my life to live over, I would place myself next to a great university and touch there tomorrow's world."

Our church a full-time instrument in the hand of God in the modern world . . . let that be our dream!

How can we bring this to pass? What will it take to make this dream come true? First we must see it. We must visualize it, behold it through the eyes of faith. It must be as real to us as this morning's sunshine that brings blossom to the buds that have waited through the snows. It must be framed in imagination and hung on the walls of our thought.

Then we must believe that it can be. Expectancy is the measure of spiritual blessing. You seldom get more than you believe in. The true Christian believes that nothing is too good to be true at the hands of God.

Then we must sacrifice for it. We must care enough to want it, investing time and talents. We do not have to be big in numbers to do this, only big in spirit. No leader here visualizes a multitudinous church, with the danger of losing the personal touch. Room for reasonable growth is our only plan. But spiritually the ceiling is unlimited. We must tithe. Tithing in stewardship, one-tenth of our income to the work of God is not too much when God makes it all possible. Sacrifice will be a pillar of this church of our dreams.

Finally, if this is to come true, we must live in the reality of it even now. We must experience it before it comes to pass. We must not build time gaps between now and then. Even now we must begin to partake of that enthusiasm and single-mindedness toward Christ that characterized the church of the New Testament, of that grandeur and mystery that dwelled even in the churches of the Middle Ages. We must feel the urgency of fulltime-ness in the modern mission of the church, penetrating every level of culture.

It will not be easy. We must let our church be the church of Jesus Christ. He belongs to the world, and the world belongs to him. No narrow, wizened view of the gospel will suffice. Ours must be a cooperative Christianity seeing friends in the faith of other name and sign; nothing less does justice to the far-flung range of eternal meanings in Christ. Our minds must be set on winning the world to him and working with all who share that purpose with us.

We must be willing to take risks for Christ, individually and corporately as a church. We must be willing to be involved in life, with all of the risks of getting hurt that love always runs. The more involved we are in life, the more real God becomes to us.

We must be willing to be interrogated by the hurt cynic, the honest seeker, the sincere doubter. Each of us must be willing to hear a gospel that chafes our pet practices, upsets our natural ways, brings us to judgment, and holds us for healing. We must be willing to spend and be spent for causes that outstrip our strength.

In an Allied prison camp in the Far East, the glad news came of Japan's surrender. Instantly, one prisoner unfurled his country's flag to the amazement of his compatriots. For three years he had hidden it upon his person at grave risk, so firm his belief in this moment of victory. He had existed in the midst of privations and struggles, but his life was set in triumph. So it must be with us.

Here is the most important thing of all: It is not up to us to make the dream come true. It is up to us to be true to the dream. This means everyone of us keeping faith with the past and with all who have labored here, keeping faith with our own destiny, and with God's will as he gives us light to see it.

This is the redemptive work to which we are called in God's name. It is a glorious task. Each one is needed. No one is strong; no one is weak. We all stand in the need of the grace of God and of one another. May each of us regard it as the ultimate compliment to have it said of him, "Behold, this dreamer cometh."

> *O God, whose strength begins where ours is no more, use us, everyone, our talents, resources, faith, even our failures. In all the joys of our belonging, let us see our responsibilities that our future may move with Thee and Thy will. Through Jesus Christ our Lord. Amen.*

Note

[1] Arthur Cleveland Coxe, *Hymns for the Living Age*, ed. H. Augustine Smith (New York: The Century Co., 1923), 446.

Meaning in Material

Joshua 4:6

(October 19, 1969)

Professor Amos Wilder has said, "A society lives by its symbols." That is true to a degree far beyond our realization. If you have shaken hands with anyone today, you have employed the accepted symbol of friendship: the clasp of a hand in another. A smile is a symbol. Even now, symbols are passing between us in communication because words are symbols; they are signs and sounds that suggest meanings.

As long as man has thought, he has developed symbols. The text today recalls the distant past when the children of Israel crossed over the Jordan into the promised land. Twelve chosen men representing all the tribes each took a stone and placed it on the bank in a heap as a memorial. Joshua declared, "When hereafter men shall ask, 'What mean ye by these stones?' You shall tell them how the waters were held back and the people passed over to the other side." The stones were an effective symbol of their wonder and gratitude to God.

Mankind still uses the language of stone, wood, metal, and glass. In so speaking, symbols do not portray meanings; they suggest meanings. The American flag pictures nothing; it stands for much,

Meaning in material . . . Jesus often used symbolic language. Of himself he said: "I am the door." "I am the shepherd." "I am the vine." Parables were a characteristic method of his teaching. Of course, the New Testament employs signs and symbols throughout, as in today's lesson from Ephesians in speaking of "the shield of faith," "the helmet of salvation," "the sword of the spirit."

Religion needs to use symbols often and well because sometimes its thought is unusual to us, or abstract, or even otherworldly. Paul Tillich has said, "One of the problems of our age is that we have no symbols that speak beyond our age." In a religious setting, symbols are instructive, inspirational, and inevitable. Yet in our churches we Baptists have tended to shy away from the use of symbols lest they become idols, objects of veneration in themselves. For fear of that, we have impoverished and deprived our worship. We have lost much in richness and vividness. We have blotted out a thoroughfare of communication and an avenue into the mind.

Now we are beginning to see that, and we like to feel that it is a mark of our maturity that we can use symbols in our houses of worship without being so foolish as to see them as anything but starting points to thought. They are not substitutes for reality. Von Ogden Vogt has said, "If you want an instrument of power, you must risk an instrument of danger, understand it, master it, and use it aright." Yes, the surgeon's knife can become the fool's weapon. Symbols are powerful and therefore dangerous. But we must take the risk. The alternative is worse. Today I shall not attempt to philosophize about symbolism in worship because next month we shall have a true authority speak to us on that subject, Dr. Horton Davies of Princeton University.

This morning, as we are becoming acquainted with our building, I should like to introduce you to just a few of the symbols to be found here. Many others you will discover yourself, perhaps using the visitor's guide that has been prepared to help you.

Long before you come anywhere near our building, from miles away there can be seen the steeple rising 183 feet above the ground. It is a silent witness to our church's being here; a pointed reference to the presence of God in the life of man. Hundreds of persons each day cannot escape seeing it. And whether they realize it or not, many will say with Proverbs, "The name of the Lord is a strong tower" (18:10).

The ridge on which we stand is a symbol. Ridge Road and River Road was a location chosen twenty-three years ago precisely because it was high ground and because it was a place where throngs of people pass on a busy road. It was never our desire to have a picturesque setting off in the woodlands. It is symbolic of this church to be in the midst of people, in the press and flow of life, and hopefully to take high ground in its values and exposure.

Our building in Colonial style bespeaks the most turbulent period in American life, but also the most productive, so far, in the amazing galaxy of great men and great ideas joined in a setting of sacrifice and idealism, believing in the rights of man as rooted in the goodness of God. It is a healthy, simple, solid, non-sentimental form in which to express our faith.

Inside our new sanctuary as you enter from the narthex, you are struck with the inspiring height of the room, the soaring of the spirit upward to behold not a flat ceiling with its suggestion of limitation and finiteness, but a rounded ceiling bending high above us as the sky itself.

The strong and majestic columns on each side bespeak beauty and strength. Through the clear antique glass, natural sunlight streams from the world without. And above each window is a frame shaped like the sun, rising "with healing in its wings," heralding a new day (Mal. 4:2).

The building inside and out is shaped like a cross, and the broad center aisle invites your eye to the very front where everything comes to a focus on the simple, unadorned cross. Recalling that God lifted up the cross to his glory to become the sign of salvation, it stands on a marble base on which is imprinted the *fleur-de-lis*, the flower of the field, with its three petals standing for the Trinity: God the Father, the Son, the Holy Spirit.

It is lighted on either side by candles recalling that Jesus is the light of the world. They stand on a *reredos*, a background for these sacred symbols, especially carved to narrow your vision from the broad room to the central point of the cross. Across the top of the *reredos* is one of the most ancient symbols known to civilization, the waves of the sea, suggesting infinity and the unending life.

In front is the table of the Lord's Supper, where, in the fellowship meal, we express our unity with one another as a church family springing from our unity with Christ, in whose sacrifice we experience the love of God for us. When we actually observe the Lord's Supper, this table will be brought out, close to all the people, a tangible cohesive object binding us to one another.

On it is the complete Bible, Old and New Testaments, telling the unfolding story of God's redemptive love. In this particular instance we are fortunate in having a rare, first edition of the King James Bible, published in 1611. The calfskin cover is a bit later, but the pages of the Bible itself are 358 years old. It was a gift to my family some years ago by friends in Baltimore who commissioned an agent in England to find it. When we think of that Bible in constant use since four years after the first English colonists sailed up the not-so-quiet James River, it adds a deep historical dimension to our worship. Many smiled indulgently when months ago I declared that we were building for at least 200 years. That becomes a tame prediction whenever we behold yonder on the Lord's Table this ancient book a century and a half older than the nation.

Also on the Lord's Table we place humbly our offerings in the bold hope that we are sharing in the sacrifices of God for a needy world and declaring our own discipleship and our stewardship of time and talent.

Flowers are there in the sanctuary, not to beautify but to proclaim God's lordship of all nature and the sacredness of all he has made. Notably the railing is without a gate; it is open to all always, reminding us of the Christian teaching that we all have "access to his grace wherein we stand." Ours is a priesthood of believers, not of a privileged few, but rather each has the sacred duty of mediating the grace of God to the others.

The stained glass window standing some fourteen feet high is, of course, seen as soon as you enter from the main door, but, purposely, you cannot make out details, only a mosaic of color. The closer you come the more you see. This in itself tells us a truth about Jesus Christ. In the three panels, each based on scripture, he is seen preaching, teaching, and healing the sick. These three activities call the contemporary church to its task: proclamation, education, and reconciliation.

From the lectern the word of God is read. From here it is interpreted by man. Our pulpit is high, not to exalt the preacher but more practically to make it easier for him to be seen and heard as he communicates with the people. Significantly, the pulpit is out where the people are, rising from the main floor of the nave. In our case, I am also glad to say that it is six-sided. From biblical days six is the number of the imperfect, the incomplete. There is no hint of perfection here. Around the top are emblems of "the shield of faith." This pulpit is altogether human although its function is holy: to interpret the word of God and to make plain its meanings for today. The canopy above is from the remote past when nothing used in worship was uncovered, not the altar or the pulpit, or for that matter the heads of the worshippers! It has survived the ages because of its practical value as a sounding board.

We must close, although there are many symbols we have not mentioned. We ask with Joshua: "What mean these stones?" What is the value of it all?

It is all a visual gate to our minds and hearts. It is meant to impress, to instruct, to create lasting images. These symbols stand between the senses and reason, a bridge of connection. They communicate the known, and declare the mysteries of the unknown; they reinforce the memories of human experience, and stimulate ideas and trains of thought. I seem to recall a word from Albert Camus to the effect that everything in life is symbolic except death.

Everything in this glorious room is intended to put us in touch with reality, not to be an escape from it. If everywhere the eye turns there is beauty, and detail that invites examination, strength that imparts strength, and straight before us a cross that "liftest up our heads"—it is because these are all attributes of God.

But the cross and the Lord's table also remind us there is sin in the world, cruelty and injustice, hardness of heart and the shedding of blood. May God grant that here we shall ever be stirred to see his strength and grace and at the same time the frailties and desperate needs of mankind—and go forth from this place with the one meeting the other.

This is the gospel. This is what it means to be church. This is what it means to have symbols not only speak to us, but also to command us.

The Story in Our Stained Glass Window

Mark 1:14; Luke 7:40, 17:15

(March 15, 1970)

Last October when we first occupied this new sanctuary we realized that we would be many, many months getting to know it in all its beauty and detail. We said then that we wanted to base a sermon sometime on the message in the stained glass window. Today we come to that subject. We have but one window of this kind. Such windows did not exist at all in the earliest colonial churches, but did come in the later period that our building represents. Then, costlier materials were available and members were more prosperous and patterns of community were more established. Even then, stained glass was used sparingly.

If from where you sit you cannot discern the figures and objects in the window, do not be dismayed. It was not intended that you should observe details from far back. This is not primarily a "picture window." It is rather a window made beautiful by the ancient craft of "staining" or coloring glass, an elaborate process of burning in the art. It is but another way of blending craftsmanship and natural elements, sun and light, to the glory of God. The intention was not to dominate the entire room, but to add luster and to complement all of the other features of the sanctuary.

Even so, though it is not primarily here to present a picture, there is a story in the window. As with our Lord himself, the closer you come the more you see. And the fresher your look the more you behold. Sunday before last the pastor's class of boys and girls standing here saw some things I had never noticed before. The window is that rich in detail. So let us look at the main story it tells.

It is called "Christ at Work, "a theme suggested and planned by a committee in our church who toiled faithfully for two years in study, travel, and supervision.

It was composed and built in the George L. Payne Studios in Patterson, New Jersey, under the direction of their leading artist Pere A. Bergethon, one of the major craftsmen in that field in America. The work is his and that of his colleagues, all coordinated by the head of the firm whose ancestor of the same name founded the firm in England in the last century.

The window was given to our church by an esteemed member, Dr. P. D. Camp, in memory of his father and mother, Mr. and Mrs. Paul D. Camp of Franklin, Virginia. We are greatly honored by this memorial because of the quality of life of these two Christians. Mr. Camp was founder of the Camp Manufacturing Company, now a major national concern, Union Camp Company. He was a leader of several related companies, but for all of his industrial and business eminence he was a humble and devout Christian. Faithful in attendance at worship, generous in support of good causes, he was a loyal friend and confidant of his pastors.

Along with many other benefactors, with his brother Mr. James Camp he established the chair of Bible at the University of Richmond. At his death in 1925, Dr. R. H. Pitt, editor of the *Religious Herald*, wrote in an editorial, "He was one of the noblest, most useful of laymen." His wife, the former Ella V. Cobb of Southampton County, was an ideal companion and homemaker and in the words of a sister-in-law paying tribute to her, "They lived a happy, peaceful, harmonious life together for forty years." This noble couple with their large family and wide interests in church, education, medicine, and community life provided us deep inspiration in planning the window and added meaning to it that will always abide.

Consider the message in the window. "Jesus came into Galilee preaching the gospel of the Kingdom of God" (Mark 1:14). Under the direction of those words our designer shows a typical scene in the preaching ministry of Jesus. He is seated in a boat on the lake of Galilee, a few feet off shore, and the people are gathered to hear him on land. Although this is an actual scene described in Scripture, the components are symbolic. The boat has been the symbol of salvation in religious history from the time of the ark of Noah, and in early Christian history it was literally the chief means of transportation and communication for the spread of the gospel among the many nations bordering the Mediterranean Sea. In the topmost panel Jesus is seen as the central figure performing the chief function of his ministry: proclaiming there is a new order in life, prepare to live in it, to be fit for it, ennobled by it, and finally to be judged by it. Jesus customarily spoke profoundly, but plainly. He moved to sweeping, sublime themes of death, victory, tragedy. In simple language, close to the vernacular, he used colorful, lively words and timely illustrations. It is no wonder that it was said of him, "The common people heard him gladly."

The second panel catches the moment when the Pharisee in whose home Jesus was visiting asked, "What is it, Teacher?" It is intended to represent the many occasions when Jesus utilized natural settings to interpret the deeper meanings of life. Everyday happenings were his curriculum, the framework on which he reconstructed the meaning of life. Here he has reacted to the Pharisee's objections to the open, demonstrative devotion of a woman known as a sinner. The Master says, "I have something to say to thee," and he begins to tell them how one who is forgiven much loves much.

As Paul Tillich has observed in a comment on this same scene, the sense of being forgiven and loved creates love. She loved because she knew God had forgiven her.

The woman in the window, as in Scripture, is carrying an alabaster flask of ointment as a sign of devotion. It is deliberately a formalized interior scene to contrast with the more casual one on the lakeshore in the panel above. The main point is to show Jesus as an authoritative teacher in a commanding position, deriving his authority from the compelling truth of his words, the vivid sincere manner in which he spoke, and the magnetic power of his personality.

There is dramatic contrast here between the two persons before him: the woman of the streets who had made her way to this house because Jesus was there and the Pharisee of impeccable reputation, the indignant host. The Pharisee had said if Jesus were a prophet, he would have known "what sort of woman she was." Jesus was not concerned with what sort of woman she was, but was concerned with her and equally with Simon the Pharisee, whose sins were just as real although of a different order.

The third and last panel is a scene more about us than about Jesus. It speaks of relationships, of human frailties, of ingratitude, of man's self-centeredness and the sincere astonishment of Jesus at the way people can turn their back on God.

Ten lepers had besought him for mercy, daring not to come close, but he in chivalry of spirit drew close to them. He told them to go on their way and they would find cleansing, and they did. In the scene one kneels at the feet of the Great Physician in gratitude and Jesus asks, "Where are the nine?" In the window they can be seen in the distance, their backs toward Jesus. Significantly in the episode reported by Luke, the one who returned is a Samaritan, not a full-fledged orthodox Jew, but a religious and racial outcast, hated and disdained by the Jews because they had intermarried with their conquerors years before and now held some views different from the main body of Jews. Yet this was the one who had the true devotion, the sense of rescue and deliverance.

The author of this gospel reportedly was Luke—whom Paul called "the beloved physician"—and our artist fittingly chose a scene from his work to depict Jesus as healer not only of the body, but also of the spirit. To this man Jesus is now saying, "Rise and go your way; your faith has made you well" (Luke 17:19).

This then is the story in our stained glass window: Jesus preaching, teaching, and healing the sick of body and of spirit. Thus we are called to the main task of the contemporary church: proclamation, education, reconciliation. The reconciliation is to be between man and man, and between man and God, the breaking down of the walls that divide us by the divine love shown in Jesus Christ.

Ours is basically a plain window in composition. There is none of the medieval aspect of transcendence, of angels ascending and descending, of stilted, kingly figures and scepters and heavenly visions. The mood is entirely different from that; it is more of our own day. The clothing is true to the period, colorful, but plain, realistic. The thrust of the message is toward us in our time, and there is no escaping the implication: Christ at work, in and through us. At the very bottom of the window between the broken arch that caps the *reredos*, again by plan, there is a crown. He is king!

May the message of this window lodge in our hearts. It must speak to us before we can carry its meanings to the world. Jesus Christ is the center of our faith; he is in every phase of existence as he is in this window. It is in the life of our Lord that we have the pattern of the meaning of existence. Our lives, as his life so fully exemplified, are to be an expression of creative and reconciling love at all levels.

God has disclosed himself to us in Jesus. In that life we find life and find God. The people in this window are divided between those who are facing him, and those who have received much and turned their backs, Where are you? Only you can decide.

O God, who came to us person to person in Jesus, we thank thee for his full and useful life, ever an inspiration to us. As we shall look upon this window of beauty and meaning, and generations after us do the same, may Christ be exalted as preacher, teacher, healer, and in our hearts given the right to rule as king. In his name. Amen.

A Church You Can Believe In

1 Peter 4:17

(October 13, 1968)

The title for our message was suggested in the remark of a youth who said with all the candor and sincerity of the young, "I want a church I can believe in."

I don't blame him! So do I! If we have a church we cannot believe in, it is a pious fraud, our spiritual life is robbed of nourishment it needs and is not likely to get elsewhere, and there will be a hole at the center of community life.

On the other hand, a church you can believe in brings great inspiration to your life and serves to enrich the community and the world. That is the kind of church we are trying to establish here. It takes time. Churches have to mature just as individuals do. We are twenty-two years old. That is a fine age, old enough to be responsible, young enough to be responsive. At twenty-two we can be flexible, romantic, a dreamer of dreams, and a doer besides.

"I want a church that I can believe in." That frankness is characteristic of youth. But it is also characteristic of the church. The remark I quoted appears in a piece of our own church school literature. "Let judgment begin at the household of God," so spoke the author of 1 Peter. The church at its best has always been austere in self-appraisal. Away back in Ezekiel where God was calling the people to judgment, he said, "Begin in the sanctuary." God always expects more of those committed to him than of anyone else. As they have been first in repentance, so they are to be first in forgiving; first in brotherly concern, in righteousness, in generosity, and in the self-examination that leads to renewal.

To begin, I am sure that we all want here a church where we will be able to believe our beliefs. They ought to be true to the message of

Scripture, for ours is an historical religion, intellectually respectable, responsibly held, subject to review in the light of new knowledge, and a witness to the whole of Christ's church—not to an isolated fragment of it.

I personally believe that ninety percent of the church's lessening power in the world is due not to increase of sin, but to decline of belief in its message. We have not taken the Bible seriously. All too often we have taken it literally—and thereby have lost its meaning.

This erosion of intellectual confidence in the Bible has been subtly at work a long time, but has reached new proportions that are like the avalanche that follows the first crumbling rocks from the mountains. P. T. Forsyth said as long ago as the first decade of this century: "The church suffers from three things: from triviality, from uncertainty of its foundation, and from satisfaction within itself."

We have a chance in this young church to study and learn the truth of the Christian message in contemporary terms, in ways that can withstand the assault of the modern mind, in ways that speak to the condition of the twentieth-century man who in his pitiable plight is like the father who stood before Christ saying, "I believe; help thou mine unbelief."

This does not mean that all belief must be reduced to the level of the rational, the plausible, the explainable, the logical. The open-minded always move among mysteries. Faith is not meant to take true mystery out of life. We may well take out superstition, hypocrisy, and futility—but not mystery.

Let us vow together to keep this church moving in the spirit of intellectual freedom, of honest inquiry, of beliefs that really mean something because they are openly arrived at and held in the confidence that God has nothing to fear from truth; he is the author of it!

A church we can believe in will not only close the credulity gap in its doctrines, but also in its program of worship, training, and outreach. That also must be something we can put our heads and hearts into.

Goethe, the German poet, has said in another connection, "The highest cannot be spoken, it can only be acted." How true! That is why we have Calvary.

If God could have reclaimed mankind, reached men's hearts, covered their sin, empowered their lives by words alone, he would surely have done it. He had said quite a bit in the Old Testament. But it took a "happening." So we have Calvary.

The church today must become a happening. There are many things that combat our becoming believable to the world, winning their respect and our own. The church is made up of people, so it is attached inseparably to the surrounding culture. It has its own built-in resistance to change. It is an institution, and always institutions tend to carry out the intent of the social order. They become caretakers of the values the social order approves.

But the church is not intended to be this kind of institution. True, it is made up of people, but it is brought into being by an act of God; it is the body of Christ in the world, bringing a divine message, living redemptively, not seeking shelter or protection from the world. Spiritually speaking, it has "nowhere to lay its head." It does not "fit in" anywhere, is "accepted" not at all in the popular sense, no more than Jesus was the young man about town, suave and soothing.

The church will become believable to the world—and to us who are within its folds—when its actions are consistent with its beliefs; when it lives like its master: dangerously, openly, sacrificially, heroically, not cowardly, timidly, unlovingly, afraid to be itself.

It is said that in the days of John Wesley in England, the archbishop of the established church looked out from his palace window and publicly bemoaned the loss of religion in his time. All the while, out where the people were, the word of God spread like a prairie fire because multitudes were finding in John Wesley's words new life and fresh awareness of the grace and power of God. I thought of that last week when I was in the British embassy in Washington for a briefing on the state of religion in the British Isles. We were told that the liveliest movements with religious implications are not in the churches. The churches are either dead or bizarre, trying to attract attention. Recently, we were told, the dean of St. Paul's jumped off the top of the cathedral in a sort of parachute contraption. John Donne, for whom the bell tolls, his predecessor by a few generations, is remembered for weightier reasons!

T. S. Eliot has said: "The church must be forever building for it is forever decaying. . . ." Yes, because it is like any live organism: When it is static, it dies.

May God grant that here our young people will not have to yearn for a church they can believe in. Rather, let them believe in this one, their own, because we are in the world to serve, to share the plight of the poor, the rejected, the unwanted. Because we are not merely trying to keep ourselves alive, we are where the action is and the need.

Finally, you will have a church you can believe in when the church can believe in you. If you want a strong church, the place to start is in being a strong member.

Nothing so weakens a church as a lack of confidence in one another. We must give good reason to be believable ourselves as Christians. Our attitudes toward our fellowmen must be quite simply like those of Christ: "Be ye kind, tender hearted, forgiving as God for Christ's sake has forgiven you." A loving life is always believable—and powerful.

It ought to make a difference in our lives to belong to a fellowship like this one—a recognizable difference. We are not a collection of saints, but a company of sinners. We are not seeking to make the church over in our image, rather to be made over in the image of God whom the church proclaims. We are not trying to get the church to endorse our way of life; on the contrary, we are trying to adopt the way of Christ whom the church presents. We are not trying to make the church believable in the sense of "ordinary." It is by nature extraordinary.

Do we not live in an unbelievable world? While we sit here this October 13, 1968, three Americans are whirling about in space, circling the globe every ninety-two minutes. They have spun around the earth once since some of us came to Sunday school this morning! And we are talking about the church being believable in a world like that! Walter Schirra was so right when he came out with that scientific observation from orbit: "It's a fantastic world up here."

Of course it is! It is down here, too. Let us not leave out the grandeur of God who is greater than our greatest thoughts of him. We don't have to be supermen—just men! There is a great future for this church on this high ground if each of us will be willing to rest his fears in God's love, and begin with himself in building beliefs that he can honestly hold, in supporting a total ministry here worthy of the world's respect, down to earth in its servanthood and willingness to touch the leper and befriend the outcast. But let it be transcendent and wondrous beyond anything this earth can afford in its luminous power as the risen Christ at work in the world. It's a tall order for mere saints of the rank and file—far beyond the strength of any one of us—but well within the competence of God.

The Environmental Crisis

Psalm 24:1

(April 5, 1970)

Mankind is undergoing an environmental crisis. Consider some of the things happening on this planet that so far as we know is the only home of man. Man has polluted his air, decimated his forests, befouled his rivers and oceans until they are heavy with his refuse, and contaminated the atmosphere with nuclear explosions. He has reproduced himself in such numbers, often uncaringly and even unwittingly, that Mother Earth can no longer sustain her progeny and must see many die who have never in fact known life.

All of this has happened so quickly in a period of other pressing problems, that twentieth-century man is just beginning to wake up to the truth that it is a rare bird that fouls his own nest and if man doesn't change his ways, there will soon not be any nest remaining.

It seems almost unbelievable, but consider a few examples that highlight the crisis. In the San Bernardino National Forest in California, more than a million ponderosa pine trees have been killed by smog that drifts in like a careless killer from the city of Los Angeles some sixty miles away. The trees, so necessary for the balance of nature, suffer chlorotic (mineral deficiency) decline, turn yellow and die. The yield of citrus fruit in the general area has been cut in half, and the raising of lettuce and spinach profitably has been eliminated altogether.[1]

Thor Heyerdahl, the author-explorer, who attempted to sail recently from Africa to Central America in a boat made of papyrus reeds, reported that "large areas even in mid-ocean were visibly polluted by human activity." Plastic bottles, squeeze tubes, tons of throwaway from our modern civilization floated by. At times the water was so dirty, they would not wash their dishes in it. In mid-ocean—1,000 miles from either shore—the crew was astonished at how man's rubbish followed them.[2]

An eminent botanist, Dr. Barry Commoner has said: "The new technological man carries strontium 90 in his bones, iodine 131 in his thyroid, DDT in his fat, and asbestos in his lungs. There is now simply not enough air, water, and soil on earth to absorb man-made poisons without effect. If we continue in our reckless way, this planet before long will become an unsuitable place for human habitation."[3]

Water is as indispensable as food. To die of hunger, one needs more than fifteen days; to die of thirst takes only three days. Yet we are squandering, polluting, and destroying water. In Los Angeles and neighboring southern California, a thousand times more water is being consumed than is being precipitated in the locality.[4]

It all comes down to the problem of population. Dr. Kenneth Vatt, a leading ecologist, says, "People have to face up to the necessity of birth control if they want freedom to move around, to be healthy, to have a balanced diet, to live like humans."[5]

Kingsley Davis, an expert on population, foresees on the basis of present trends that a child born today will live to see the number of people to be fed and housed at 15 billion—nearly five times as many as today. Under the same trend, in 55 years 100 percent of the world's population will be living in cities, and the largest city will be 186 times as large as Greater London today.[6]

One of those largest cities will touch us; it is already being called by the experts "Bowash," a continuous city from Boston to Washington, one vast swarming mass of humanity, and gradually spreading on down the Atlantic seaboard in a broad swath to the tip of Florida.[7]

Lord Ritchie-Calder, a distinguished science journalist, takes a hard, discouraging look at the way man has taxed his habitat to the utmost limits and speaks for most knowledgeable persons in this field when he says, "We have mortgaged the old homestead, and nature is liable to foreclose."[8]

Does all of this have anything to do with religion, or is it purely a scientific matter that can be left to the experts to solve?

If you listened carefully to the biblical readings this morning, you will know that it has a great deal to do with religion. "The earth is the Lord's and the fullness thereof; the world and those that dwell therein"

(Ps. 24:1). If that is true, then it is somebody's else property we are befouling, abusing, poisoning, and destroying—God's! If these very lives of ours are his, then it is his children we are corrupting, dehumanizing, and wasting; bringing them into existence often unwanted, unloved, and in many areas of the world left to starve.

The word ecology is new to many persons. It stems from a Greek word *oikos* meaning "house." Ecology is the study of nature's housekeeping. It is the scientific observation of the interdependence of life, the balance of processes that keeps all forms of life vital.

Long before there was such a word or such a science there was Jeremiah speaking for God: "I brought you into a plentiful country, to eat the fruit thereof and the goodness thereof; but when you entered you defiled my land, and made mine heritage an abomination" (Jer. 2:7). Throughout the times of the prophets they thundered their reminders that God had brought his children out of a land of deserts and drought to a land "flowing with milk and honey." The contrast was ever before them. It represented God's kind providence. Yet, as here in the passage from Jeremiah, the people so easily forgot and even made the richness of the earth an occasion for idolatry, the ultimate desecration! There is, indeed, throughout the Bible a close connection between the defilement of the earth and its resources and the wrath of God, the revulsion of nature and of nature's God.

What are we to do? First, we are to be aware of the problem, to wake up and live in order to let live.

Second, we are to take personal responsibility. This extends from "Don't be a litterbug" all the way to big business and industry that must be willing to sacrifice profits for vast expenditures to stop pollution and stem the tide of filth racing through our airways and waterways. Some persons very superficially have said that environmental control is a popular topic, thrown up to take our minds off other pressing social problems. This is far off the mark. Wait until the public is aroused and laws are passed and enforced that hit the pocketbook of all of us, and you will see the most unpopular issue in American life. We should prepare now to see that this is not only a matter of public interest, but also of survival itself, requiring the utmost in character, discipline, and concern for the general welfare.

Third, each of us can relate this whole matter to his Christian faith because we have a mandate from God to protect the earth, "to replenish it." In the words of theologian Joseph Sittler, the earth is "the theater of God's grace."[9]

Long before that, John Calvin said to anyone who owned a field: "Let him so feed on its fruits, that he neither dissipates it by luxury, nor permits it to be . . . ruined by neglect. . . . Let everyone regard himself as the steward of God."[10]

Friends, it is later than we think. Thousands of years have passed since some of these biblical warnings were first uttered. Civilization has not only grown; it has aged. It is no longer in the morning of its youth, reckless and spendthrift. Civilization is in a phase of its development where it must recycle, renew, reuse, and learn to live under a sacramental view of all its resources. That means a view of life that sees natural resources as a means of grace.

They are of God. The grace of God, the undeserved favor of God upon our lives, is most vividly expressed to be sure in a person like unto us, yet without sin—Jesus Christ. God's own likeness, we believe, is disclosed in him. But nature also is the creation of God, and for the good of man, and therefore it conveys divine grace.

The theologians and the scientists have combined to convince us that all spheres of life are fused, intermingled, interdependent, not susceptible to being separated as the natural world from the human world. It is one creation.

Nature is not merely mechanistic, devoid of grace, threatening to spirit, subhuman. On the contrary it is responsive to the common ground of relationships. There is "a hint of continuity" that runs through all structures of existence. This is the big fact for us to contemplate and act upon: the unity of creation, of all God's creatures, human and otherwise, and the dependence of all the creatures upon the order of nature. Through it all there runs "a good not our own, an intimation of the More to be received."[11] It all bespeaks the wonder and glory of God beneath whose love we live. It all points to the meaning of existence, for the chief end of man is to glorify God and to enjoy him forever.

O God before whose face the generations rise and fall, help us to see with ever increasing clarity that we humans are a part of all thou has made, and we are dependent upon the unity we deny in our greed and haste. Give us a sacramental view of material things that in just proportion and in due humility we may use and not abuse. In the name of Christ our Lord. Amen.

Notes

[1] *American Forest*, April 1970, 16f.
[2] *Time*, August 16, 1969, 40.
[3] Ibid.
[4] *Sports Illustrated*, February 2, 1970.
[5] *Time*, 51.
[6] *Sports Illustrated*, February 2, 1970, 51.
[7] Ibid.
[8] Ibid.
[9] Joseph Sittler, *The Care of the Earth* (Philadelphia: Fortress Press, 1964), 51.
[10] John Calvin, *Calvin's Commentaries*, Genesis, vol. 1 (Grand Rapids: Wm. B. Eerdmans Publishing Co., 1948), 125, quoted in E. T. Campbell, "Meanwhile—Back on Earth" (New York: Riverside Church, July 1969).
[11] Philip J. Hefner, ed., *The Scope of Grace* (Philadelphia: Fortress Press, 1964), 160.

For Further Reading

Ehrlich, Paul. *The Population Bomb*. New York: Ballentine Books, 1968.
Ehrlich, Paul and Anne H. "The Food from the Sea Myth." *Saturday Review*, April 4, 1970, 53f.
Fagley, Richard M. *The Population Explosion and Christian Responsibility*. New York: Oxford University Press, 1960.
"Cleaning Humanity's Nest." *Saturday Review*, March 7, 1970, 47-61; see bibliography, 61.
"The Oceans, Man's Last Great Resource." *Saturday Review*, October 11, 1969, 19f.

Life on Leftovers

Acts 27:43-44

(November 29, 1970)

In the light of the fact that this is the Sunday after Thanksgiving and every home among us has survived on leftovers from the big Thursday meal, the title of my message may seem trivial: "Life on Leftovers." Other than that connection, which is not entirely coincidental, this is a serious theme worthy of our attention.

One of the real tests of character is how you handle the rest of life when it has been reduced to pieces and fragments—leftovers. You remember the lines of the Scottish poet Robert Burns as he turned up a field mouse's dwelling with the plow: "The best laid schemes of mice and men gang aft a-gley." (They go awry.) "And leave us nought but grief and pain for promised joy."[1]

When things go awry and not as you had planned, what do you do with the leftovers? When the waters of life roll over you like heavy seas over a broken ship, what then?

Our lesson of scripture is Acts of the Apostles, chapter 27, the vivid story of Paul's shipwreck in the Mediterranean Sea on the way to Rome to preach the gospel in the center of the civilized world. I used to dislike this particular chapter in seminary because of the unusual vocabulary in it, quite different from anything else in the New Testament, many technical words of nautical origin. It is authentic sea-going language. I took Greek in a class of two. There was no question about whether you would be called upon to translate, only whether you would have the first one-half hour or the second one-half hour of the period! This particular chapter was a real stumper. Previous experience counted for nothing. Anyway, this is only by way of saying that the author told a dramatic story of rough winds, high seas, black night, foodless days, a frightful voyage that ended with the ship going aground off the island of Malta. The chapter ends with these words: "He (the military commander) ordered those who could swim to throw themselves overboard first and make for the land, and the rest on planks or on pieces of the ship. And so it was that all escaped to land."

Consider in the first place that taken in the figurative sense this is pretty nigh a universal experience. Most of us get through the voyage of life not as a pleasure cruise but quite often overboard, clinging to planks and broken pieces of the ship. But we make it!

Life seldom turns out just as we had planned it. The biblical faith continually reminds us of the uncertainties of existence. Its historical portions begin with Abraham of whom it was said, "He went out not knowing whither he went." The book of James in the New Testament says, "Ye know not what shall be in the morrow" (4:14).

Some of the greatest life stories of our day are of those people who, having seen their ship wrecked on the shallows, have made their way triumphantly on broken pieces that remained.

A few weeks ago having a speaking engagement in Urbana, I went by Saluda to inquire about the health of my friend Major General Chesty Puller, the most decorated man in Marine Corps history. I not only learned that he was improving from a recent illness, but also heard about his son. This splendid young man is studying law at the College of William and Mary. But he did not get there with easy sailing. In Vietnam he lost both legs and sustained a serious injury to his hand. But there he is! An ebullient and indomitable spirit, calling out to anyone who tends to go glooming over him: "Don't pity me. I'm getting along fine."

"Clinging to planks and broken pieces of the ship, they all escaped to land."

Dr. Dewitt Talmage, a famous minister of three generations ago, in the home of whose grandson I lived for three years, used to read this chapter to couples about to marry with the reminder that life's venture seldom turns out exactly as you plan it and that the deep waters hold hidden dangers, but that with God's help and our courage we can come through victoriously.

Consider secondly that life on leftovers, making the most of what remains, is not only a universal experience demanded of practically all of us, but that with our purposes entrusted to God the planks and broken pieces—the wreckage of our hopes and plans—can be the very instrument of our rescue and salvation. The Apostle Paul had complete trust that the ship would not carry him to his death because he believed so strongly that God had work for him to do in Rome.

In a secular sense this was true of General Charles de Gaulle, whose death occurred a few days ago after an amazing career that really began when France collapsed in 1940 and broke into a thousand pieces. I was living in England as a student when that occurred. Equally amazing to me were the words and the spirit of Prime Minister Winston Churchill when he learned that France, the principal ally, had surrendered. I thought he would be furious and disgusted. Yet so firmly did Mr. Churchill believe in the eventual triumph of his cause that with Dunkirk, the darkest day of the war staring him in the face, here is what he broadcast to the French people and for his own people to hear as France went into the hands of the enemy:

> Good night then. Sleep to gather strength for the morning. For the morning will come. Brightly will it shine on the brave and true, kindly upon all who suffer for the cause, glorious upon the tombs of heroes. Thus will shine the dawn. *Viva la France.*[2]

"And so on planks and on broken pieces of the ship they all escaped to land."

The loss of France, the miracle of rescue of the hundreds of thousands of British soldiers at Dunkirk brought home safely in small boats on strangely quiet waters of the usually rough English channel, brought a new unity and deepened purpose to the people of Britain, won them new allies and final victory. In a secular sense, I say, it is an illustration of how broken pieces, dashed hopes, fragments, are often the very instruments of rescue and salvation.

How about in a spiritual sense? I may be talking to someone here today for whom life has gone on the rocks. First plans, preferred expectations, have run afoul of stormy weather. And if you make it to shore at all, it will have to be on "planks and broken pieces of the ship."

Do two things. Make sure by prayer that the direction and destination of your life is as clearly within the purposes of God as Rome was for Paul. He found a booming, buoyant confidence in that he had a great work to do. And then trust the loving mercies and wisdom of God to make even wreckage—the leftovers—an instrument of rescue and salvation,

You can come through stronger and more useful to him than ever. Not necessarily happier in the human definition; that is not the chief purpose of life anyway. But more use to God; that is the chief purpose of life.

Isn't this among the things God is trying to tell us in Christ? That his grace is sufficient for us. That he can make the wrath of man to praise him. That nothing can happen to us that God cannot use for our good and his glory. The cross—the plank and broken piece of Jesus' own personal desires, not his first choice at all—is the sign of salvation to all who take the way of sacrifice and love. This is God's word to all of us who, starting in high expectation, must live with what remains. With God's help, even that can be a victory.

Notes

[1] Robert Burns, "To a Mouse, on Turning Her Up in Her Nest, with the Plough," *Anthology of the World's Best Poems*, vol. 3, selected by Edwin Markham (New York: Wm. H. Wise Co., 1950), 1325.

[2] *Churchill Remembered*, BBC Audio, 2006. See also www.winstonchurchill.org/support/The Churchill-Centre.

James Hoyt Slatton
(Pastor, 1971-2003)

James Hoyt Slatton was born in Fort Worth, Texas, on January 15, 1933, the son of H. S. (Pete) Slatton and Mary Sue Rumph. His mother died when Slatton was only five years old. A few years later his father, who was a funeral director and an embalmer, remarried and moved eventually to Dallas, where he founded the Slatton-Hughes Funeral Home.

In his senior year at Adamson High School in Dallas, Texas, Slatton won the National Forensic League's national high school championship in debating. Feeling a "call to preach" in high school, he attended Baylor University on a four-year debating scholarship. In college he was a varsity debater for four years and was elected to *Pi Kappa Delta*, the national honorary speech fraternity, and to Who's Who in American Colleges and Universities in 1952-53 and 1953-54. He also participated in the youth revival movement current in those years. During this period, in a revival meeting in Ocean View Baptist Church in Norfolk, Virginia, he met Elberta Lee Thornton, an accomplished pianist, who later became his wife.

After graduating from Baylor University in 1954, Slatton went to Southwestern Baptist Theological Seminary in Fort Worth, Texas, where he received the B.D. degree in 1957 and the Th.D. degree in 1965. His doctoral dissertation was on "Early American Baptist Concepts of the Separation of Church and State." During college and part of his first year in seminary, he was pastor, from 1951-1954, of a "quarter time" church, Fate Baptist Church in Fate, Texas. In his seminary years, he was student pastor of South Lancaster Baptist Church in Dallas, Texas, from 1954-1960. He was pastor of the First Baptist Church of Altavista, Virginia, from 1960-1967. And from 1967-1971, he was pastor of the Royal Lane Baptist Church in Dallas, Texas.

On June 21, 1956, Dr. Slatton married Elberta Lee Thornton, and they have three children and two grandchildren. Lee graduated from Baylor University with a B.A. degree. As a nationally accredited piano teacher, Lee maintained a studio at home teaching piano. She moreover served as interim choral director at First Baptist Church, Altavista, while her husband was pastor there.

James Slatton was called from Royal Lane to serve as pastor of the River Road Church in 1971. He remained as pastor for thirty-one years until he retired on his seventieth birthday in 2003. During his ministry the church completed several building projects, including the addition of a large brick plaza and the front driveway, the complete development of the two major parking lots, a new church kitchen, a columbarium for the committal of human ashes, a $5 million remodeling and renovation of the existing church buildings, and the addition of a fourth educational and music facility. During his tenure the church also reached it first million-dollar budget, elected its first women deacons, had a note-burning ceremony for the church sanctuary mortgage, installed a new organ for the chapel, installed an elevator, established the Board of Christian Education, and established a Denominational Affairs Committee to monitor the Southern Baptist Convention crisis.

While serving as pastor, Dr. Slatton also served as a trustee on the boards of Virginia Baptist Hospital, Golden Gate Baptist Theological Seminary, the University of Richmond, Virginia Baptist Foundation,

Baptist Theological Seminary at Richmond, and the Board of Associates of the University of Richmond. He has also served on the Executive Committee and General Board of the Baptist General Association of Virginia. From 1975-1976, he was president of the Richmond Area Clergy Association. For two years he served as the national chair of the moderate Baptist organization during the SBC controversy. He served from 1991-1996 on the Coordinating Council of the National Cooperative Baptist Fellowship and was chair of that organization's personnel committee. He was a member of Virginia Baptists Committed from the outset. He was appointed by Governor Gerald Baililes to serve on the Virginia-Israel Commission.

In 1985 Dr. Slatton was given an honorary Doctor of Divinity degree by the University of Richmond. The *Richmond Magazine* named him in its March 1998 edition as one of "The Region's 100 Power Players." He was also selected in 2003 to be in the "Mainstream Baptist Hall of Fame." Since retiring, he has served on occasions as an adjunct professor at the Baptist Theological Seminary at Richmond and was "a scholar-in-residence at the Virginia Baptist Historical Society. From this research came Dr. Slatton's first book, *W. H. Whitsitt: The Man and the Controversy*, published by Mercer University Press in 2009.

Over the years he has contributed articles to magazines such as *Journal for Preaching, Lectionary Homiletics*, and *Now*, and to the following book collections: *Preaching the Baptist Vision of the Priesthood of Believers, The Struggle for the Soul of the SBC, Invitation to Dialogue-Professional Ethics*, and *History of River Road Church, Baptist, 1946-1996*. In 2010 he appeared as a commentator on the role of Virginia Baptists in the struggle for religious freedom and the separation of church and state in America on a PBS documentary produced by WGBH Boston called *God in America*. Dr. Slatton continues, as there is opportunity and time, to preach, teach, and write, as well as support the ministry of River Road Church.

The Word, Divine and Human

John 1:1, 14

(July 8, 1979)

My sermon this morning is prompted by developments in the life of our denomination. As many of you by now are aware, there was, in Houston, in June, at the gathering of the Southern Baptist Convention, a highly organized political effort by a subgroup to dominate the meeting. This group was successful in electing its candidate as president. It was not successful in doing some other things—one of which was to impose upon all agency appointees, officers of the convention, and professors of theological seminaries a very rigid confession of faith. The press described the group as conservative. That is really a misnomer.

To speak plainly, the group is fundamentalist, as in the classic fundamentalism of J. Gresham Machen and the Fundamentalist-Modernist controversy of the 1920s. Theirs is the same kind of fundamentalism that gave us the Scopes trial and was discredited publicly by that famous trial in Tennessee. Fundamentalism did not disappear or go away. It simply lost center stage to other things, such as the Great Depression, the Second World War, and the postwar boom. Fundamentalism persisted and has grown. It survives in significant numbers in our own denomination.

To seize center stage in Houston, the fundamentalists dragged out and trumpeted one of their major dogmas: biblical inerrancy—the assertion the Bible is infallible. Because they have now brought this issue to the forefront in the SBC, and because we need to be honest and forthright with each other in our own church about our use of the Bible, I want to talk with you today about how we handle the Bible. Unfortunately, this particular issue probably will not be met head on at the denominational level. It is too loaded a term. To deny the "inerrancy" of the Bible can sound even as bad as attacking motherhood or the flag. But, here at least, I want to deal with it.

We must begin by acknowledging our common ground with the fundamentalists at least in the great concern that underlies their inerrancy doctrine. They are concerned that everyone recognizes the importance of the Bible. We share their concern and are unwilling to take a backseat to anyone in our devotion to Scripture. Here, of course, is the irony of the Bible dispute. The ultimate danger is neither from the left or right within the churches. The real threat is disuse of the Scriptures within our whole society. Fundamentalists try to accomplish their purpose by insisting the Bible is literally without error of any kind. If biblical infallibility were a reliable approach to the Bible, I would be the first to go along with them. Unfortunately, the infallibility or inerrancy of the Scriptures sounds good, trips well across the tongue, and pours pious praise all over the Bible. But it fails as an accurate or even useful description of the way biblical authority works. In fact, the inerrancy dogma often produces just the opposite effect. All too often a militant fundamentalist take on the Bible makes the Christian faith seem ridiculous and outdated to modern people.

Even if we grant, for the sake of discussion, that the Bible is inerrant, we still have the task of understanding what it is actually saying and of comprehending what it means by what it says. As soon as we ask what a text really says and means, we are already into the area of interpretation. Right there is where inerrantists "drop their candy," because however perfect the Bible, interpretation and application are the tasks of fallible human beings.

Have you noticed, as I have, that people who claim the Bible is inerrant tend to extend inerrancy and infallibility not only to the Scriptures, but also to their own interpretations? I don't think I would mind so much if a person claimed infallibility for the Bible—but then admitted that what he understood the Bible to say was only his own opinion, and very much subject to error. The trouble is, most people begin with an inerrant Bible and end with infallible opinions about the Bible.

If the Bible is inerrant, must we take the account of the creation of the Earth in six days to mean six literal twenty-four-hour periods? Or, can we interpret that as symbolic, the language of profound imagery? Does an inerrant Bible force us to fit the whole history of the human race into a timeline determined by the genealogies of the Bible and the sequence of Bible events, as Bishop Ussher did in the seventeenth century, and as many biblicists do right up to the present day?

By their lights, an inerrant Bible compresses the age of earth and humankind to so small a package—as little as 6,000 years—they are compelled to deny findings like that of the expedition in Africa that has recently unearthed a hominid bone three million years old. Such resistance to the discoveries of modern science in the name of Bible faith has been going on for a long time. When Darwin discovered in the arroyos of the South American pampas huge prehistoric, fossilized bones, the local inhabitants insisted that the fossil bones grew after death. And they said that certain rivers "have the powers of making small bones into large bones."[1]

Does an inerrant Bible demand we admire as the will of a just God injunctions demanding destruction of captives, or the stoning of people offending particular codes of ancient Hebrew society, even when we no longer feel bound by those injunctions ourselves? If the viewpoint of the writers of the Old Testament is that the earth is the center of the universe, does this mean we must believe in a three-storied universe, with heaven up and the underworld down and the middle story made up of a flat earth?

If, as we read in the Book of Acts, people in the early church were required to pool their possessions and have all things in common, are we as churchmen required to practice communal communism as well. If not, why not? If Jesus said to the rich man, "give all that you have to the poor and come follow me," does this mean that in Christianity every rich man must give away all he has? And if Jesus said that it is easier for a camel to go through the eye of a needle than for a rich man to enter the kingdom of God, does this mean that the chances at the front office are very slim for the prosperous? If Jesus washed his disciples' feet and said that anyone who did not participate had no part in him, why are we free not to take him literally, making foot washing an ordinance of the church?

You see what I mean! By the way, which Bible is infallible? The Revised Standard Version or the King James? For they differ! How about the Douay Confraternity version of the Roman Catholics? What about Luther's German Bible? What about the Greek New Testament of Erasmus of Rotterdam? What about the fact that there are many surviving fragments of the New Testament—some large, some small, some older than others—that differ among themselves? For instance, in the earliest witnesses the familiar account about Jesus and the woman who was taken in adultery is either not in the Gospel of John at all or placed elsewhere (sometimes in the Gospel of Luke).[2] Which fragment of the New Testament is infallible?

The fundamentalists at our convention took the position that the original manuscripts of the books of the Bible are the infallible ones. The problem is that no one today—or for countless centuries—has seen the original manuscripts. They are lost and may no longer exist. Quotations of New Testament texts by writers of the early church period are some of the earliest witnesses we now have to what might be in original documents. If you consider the Old Testament—Exodus or Genesis, for instance—the story of how the texts come down to us goes something like this, if I'm reading the experts correctly.

Our texts began with stories originating long before they were written, were repeated orally around campfires over a long stretch of time, eventually were put into writing, and eventually were incorporated into larger collections. Along the way the manuscripts were edited, perhaps repeatedly into the books we now have. Where, along the way, does one find the originals, the "autographs" as they are called? The problem is that the concept of infallibility doesn't serve us very well. What it does serve is the practice of identifying one's own mental pictures of biblical events with the events themselves. So the mental images one has of the creation, exodus, tower of Babel, and so on are taken to be what the Bible says and what the Bible really means, and are invested with a quality of inerrancy.

Another problem with infallibility, it seems to me, is that it fails to adequately regard the difference between the word and the words. I refer to "the word" in the sense John was getting at in his gospel when he wrote, "In the beginning was the word, and the word was with God . . ." That word, Word with a capital W, describes an ultimate meaning, the very mind and intention of God's own self, transcendent truth. When John speaks of that "word that was with God and was God," he clearly is not talking about mere verbiage or printed words. Our words on the other hand are at best limited, partial. They refer, describe, point beyond themselves. Inevitably, they distort as well as represent.

To put a message into words is to confine it to words and, as it were, to reduce it to a kind of shorthand. The Bible, of course, is made up of words, human words, finite words. They are pressed into service to convey the message of God and the meaning of human life. There is a distinction between the many little human words, even the ones used in the Bible, and the word. If you impute infallibility to the words, you may very well confuse them with the great word toward which they point, the great word they never completely contain. The text then is no longer a window through which we look beyond toward the word that was with God.

Literalism, which is the Siamese twin of inerrancy, too easily misses the character of religious language. Philip Wheelwright in his book, *The Burning Fountain*, made the distinction between depth language, "the language of the full song," and "steno-language" that he called the language of science and precise logical description. As Horace Bushnell said, all religious language is metaphorical. It is depth language; it tries to say the things of heaven in the words of earth. It has the quality of poetry, of metaphor, of figure of speech. To take the Bible seriously is never the same thing as to take it literally. I advocate taking it seriously. I do not advocate taking it with flat-footed and wooden-headed literalness. John never said the word became print; he said "the Word became flesh." It has always taken imagination to get what a religious story is all about.

I am concerned, not merely with the difference in points of view that I have tried to address here. I am worried by the spirit of this present controversy. The intent of the fundamentalists is to use inerrancy as a slogan and battle flag in a campaign for religious power. They are using it as a divisive issue to discredit, disempower, and disenfranchise those who do not stand with them. Their fellow travelers they call godly and Bible-believing Christians. Those who do not follow them they call liberals and heretics who do not believe the Bible.

I really think where inerrancy and fundamentalism do their greatest damage is in distorting the process by which people make the journey of faith. We must all find the truth for ourselves. We must think it through. We must be free to say yes or no, even to imagine different alternatives. Truth is never truth wrapped in cellophane and handed out predigested. Well, it often is, actually, but you should not swallow it whole that way. Religious truth cannot be kept rightly as cold propositional formulas to be accepted without question. Religious truth is never true really until it is true for you.

A friend of mine, Bill Martin, was scheduled to act as a driver for the famous theologian Paul Tillich after one of his lectures in Chicago. Just as Tillich was making his way toward Bill and his waiting automobile that evening, a young man in a blue suit with a black leather Bible suddenly appeared and intercepted the professor. Holding the Bible out, almost under Tillich's nose, and with anger in his voice he demanded: "Professor Tillich, do you believe this to be the word of God?" Tillich said quietly, "Yes, if it grasps you, but not if you are grasping it." Therein lies the essential difference! The truth becomes the truth when, as Samuel Taylor Coleridge put it, "the Bible finds me."

Just here I have to watch my own step. I do not wish to fall into the same trap that I am condemning. The trouble begins when we see the problem as being out there in the other fellow. That is the very thing our fundamentalist friends have been doing. Let me remind myself, and you, of what I am supposed to have learned through many years of pastoral practice and some good reading. Whenever one gets all worked up about someone else's sins, when the bad guys are all out there somewhere and the problem is them, you may be sure he/she is not facing something inside herself/himself. "Scapegoating" is the most eloquent confession of unresolved guilt known to man. So what is bugging the fundamentalists?

It is the same thing that bothers all of us. It is scary to have to process truth and error and decide which is which. It is scary to be like Adam in the Garden of Eden, with God walking in the cool of the day, calling out, "Adam where art thou?" There, each of us must sort out from among all the clamorous witnesses and claims and voices of the day the true voice and decide what must be believed and not believed, what must be done and not done.

To decide and to act in response to God is always a scary business. Like Adam, you are all by yourself, and you have to decide. Wouldn't it be so much nicer if the church could come thundering in with massive and overwhelming authority and simply tell you what to do? Ah! What a relief it would be not to be responsible anymore. It has never been the task of the church to think for us or even to tell us what to think. It is ever the task of the church to point to what is worth thinking about. So, my fellow Adams, in the cool of the evening when God walks in the garden and you have to hear and respond for yourself, I will be thinking about you. I'll even pray for you. What I will not do is try to decide for you!

Notes

[1] Loren Eiseley, *Darwin and the Mysterious Mr. X* (New York: E. P. Dutton, 1979) 6.

[2] *New English Bible* (New York: Oxford University Press), 143, n.1.

(Dr. Slatton delivered this sermon shortly after the meeting of the Southern Baptist Convention in 1979 in Houston, Texas, to inform the congregation about the use of the terms infallibility and inerrancy of the Bible by the fundamentalist group in the convention in their efforts to "take over" the convention and establish the belief in inerrancy and infallibility as essential for authentic Baptist beliefs.)

For Such a Time as This

(September 16, 2001)

The overwhelming reality within which we meet for worship today is the devastating attacks on the Twin Towers and the Pentagon this past Tuesday. I have heard no one capture the impact of this tragedy better than a twelve-year-old girl whose words I found in the newspapers this week:

> I could never have imagined anything of this magnitude in the U.S. When I saw the plane hit the second tower, [the] bubble I had been living in popped. In an instant the world was real, threats of wars and bombings suddenly so much closer. When the towers went down, I thought it had to be a dream. I thought I'd wake up and everything would be OK. But I didn't wake up, and it wasn't a dream. . . . When the Pentagon was hit, it was terrifying it was so close to home. I thought that if New York, the largest city in the country, and the Pentagon, the military base for all of America, weren't safe, what was? I'm just a kid, but on September 11, it felt as though I grew up in one horrendous hour.

The bubble popped indeed. If those massive and iconic buildings at the center of the greatest of our cities and the military headquarters in our nation's capital were not safe, then "what was"? I don't think the question can be better put. I have a sick feeling in the pit of my stomach that has not gone away since Tuesday. I don't know when it will. Perhaps you feel the same.

The words of the prophet Isaiah, uttered so many centuries ago, seem to leap the intervening centuries into our own moment. "The foundations of the earth do shake, Earth breaks to pieces, Earth is split in pieces, Earth shakes to pieces . . . To rise no more!" Indeed! If his description of the shaking of the very foundations of our world expresses our sense of things here and now, perhaps his resounding affirmation can be a word from the Lord as well: "The world itself shall crumble, But my righteousness shall be forever, And my salvation knows no end" (Isa. 24:18-20).

So timely, also, seem the words of the Apostle Paul in this morning's epistle reading. He begins by wishing the church joy in the Lord. Not exactly our first sentiment at this moment! Urging his readers to be magnanimous, he next offers what sounds like impossible advice: "Do not be anxious." Do not be anxious? Instead he advises, "Let your requests be made known to God in prayer." That is more like it. Many of us found ourselves resorting to prayer all unbidden this week. Finally, says Paul, "The peace of God, which is beyond all understanding, will guard your hearts and your thoughts in Christ Jesus" (Phil. 4:4-6).

But first, grief . . .

I think where we have to begin today is with grief. Whatever else we have come to do, we have come to grieve: to mourn those who were lost in the planes crashed into buildings and into the earth; to mourn the unsuspecting victims in those great office towers and at the Pentagon; to mourn those who died trying to help them—firefighters, rescue workers, medical and emergency people. John Donne was right: "Any man's death diminishes me because I am involved in Mankind / And therefore never send to know for whom the bell tolls / It tolls for thee."[1]

No one is a rock or an island alone. We are all part of one single humanity, bone of their bone, flesh of their flesh. Every one of those deaths cuts into us. We must mourn brothers and sisters whose faces and names we will never know.

As the twelve-year-old girl's letter so poignantly states, we mourn not only the dead. We mourn also the loss of something more. Not only have we lost fellow Americans, sister human beings, we have lost something else, something we had a moment before and now possess no longer. We have lost something both intangible but also quite real. Call it "the way things were." Call it a "way of looking at things" or "a way of life." It is as if a state of being went down in the same erupting cloud of destruction with those great buildings and their human victims. In the words of Isaiah, the earth is shaken to pieces to rise no more. What seems lost, and what we have begun to mourn, is a sense of freedom and security in which we moved about just a few short days ago.

That young girl's letter took my mind back to a time when, like her, I was a child of twelve. The year was 1945, very near the end of the Second World War. I heard one day a radio broadcast describing the use of a powerful new bomb on a city in Japan. They called it an atomic bomb. It was so powerful, it could wipe out a whole city in a single blast. I understood at once that this was no ordinary event. If there was now a weapon that could vaporize cities in the blink of an eye, that clearly changed everything. A shiver went through me that I can still recall. Many of you remember! Our whole world passed under the shadow of a mushroom cloud.

Perhaps in the excitement of the moment I am blowing things out of all proportion here. Maybe in some better-or-worse future we will look back on this September and see this horror less earthshaking than it now seems. But at the moment I truly believe we're in the midst of another "existential shock," not as big as the breaking forth of the nuclear age, perhaps, but certainly another shaking of the very foundations; another "sea change," not only in world and national affairs, but also in our national psyche. I fear it is one that does not bode well for us or for our future. Such a passage calls forth grief and tears over what we have lost. We've come to mourn a while.

A few words about grief seem in order. Our losses must be appropriated. We must allow them to "sink in." That is what grief is, the painful process of letting losses become so real we can begin to make peace with them. In the journey called grief we actually withdraw, over time, the emotional investment of ourselves we have made in someone or something we've loved and lost. As we do so, we are enabled gradually to reinvest ourselves in new loves and new commitments. Grief is the gradual and painful move from what was to what is and what is yet to be. So, dear friends, scarcely able to keep ourselves together, we have come together to mourn as we sing these great hymns and lift up our prayers of love for our nation and devotion to God.

Another part of grieving is the struggle to get our minds around a loss. We are hungry to understand what has happened. We want answers. In the face of last Tuesday we have a million questions. How did this come to be? Who were those people who flew airliners into buildings? What did they hope to accomplish? We think if we can only know more fully, we might find some way to regain control of what is happening to us. Perhaps if we could understand, we could reduce a horrifying reality to manageable proportions. At least with better understanding, we might reduce the pain.

Grieving, we instinctively seek some kind of "closure." We feel the need to pull things together. If only we could pull together all the broken pieces of the tragedy, wrap up all the chaotic parts of the disaster, we might find our way to some kind of resolution. Then we could pronounce a benediction over it all and begin to move on. Unfortunately, especially at this early stage, we sense no resolution. We cannot even imagine a satisfying closure. No worthy benediction comes to mind. That huge mass of wreckage in New York, the wound in the side of the Pentagon, and that scarred field where the last airliner bit into the earth—all are open wounds.

One of the moods of grief, of course, is anger and rage. Our lives have been broken into and violated. Our safety has been threatened—perhaps for the rest of our lives. We are enraged! This country has terrible power. When that power is awakened, it is awesome beyond description—and dangerous. Once again the sleeping giant has been awakened.

I was at lunch this week with some respected companions. As you would expect, we were talking about this very matter. It happened that one of my friends, an elderly physician, was a Yale man and the son of Presbyterian missionaries in Egypt. He was born in Egypt, spent his earliest youth in Cairo, spoke fluent Arabic, and cherished an enduring love for the region and its people. I asked him what he thought the terrorists were trying to accomplish. Almost without pause he answered, "They wanted revenge. They wanted revenge." I couldn't help but say, "But revenge is a dead end. Revenge is a dead end." He nodded in silent and frustrated agreement.

It is a frightening new world. We grieve our losses. Grief has many moods, and one of them is rage, the rage we feel right now. Rage is inevitable and must be entertained. It belongs to grief, but it is just one of the moods of grief. Sometimes rage issues in a quest for revenge, but the wisdom of our faith through the ages is that revenge is a dead-end street. Revenge is not the answer. It must not be our answer.

A matter of the eternal . . .

Whatever else these events are about, they confront us with religious and faith issues. The people involved in the plot made it clear they saw their act as bidden and sanctioned by God. They drove the airliners into their unsuspecting targets with prayers and praise to their God on their lips. Evidently they believed passionately their targets were God's targets and they themselves martyrs with certain and instant passes admitting them to paradise as the eternal reward of their unspeakable deeds. Suddenly, religion no longer seems the harmless diversion many people seem to think. The difference between good religion and bad no longer seems merely academic. Our hands have been called on who God is and what God wants of us.

As we've already heard, Isaiah says that when the foundations we've depended upon and trusted are shaken, when those things we've put our hopes in are shattered, we are forced to reach out for that which remains. Can there be any doubt the question of this week's events is essentially a religious question? Is it not clear we are thrown back upon some serious theological work? At stake is the vision of God. Who is God and what does God require of us?

You may remember the widely viewed and highly praised series of televised conversations between Bill Moyers and the renowned professor of world religions, Joseph Campbell. In that dialogue there was a moment when Campbell mused on the religious imperative to love one another. He said he found the love teaching to be central and common to virtually all of the world's great religious traditions. The problem, said Campbell, is that the devotees of those religions too often apply the demand to love one another only to their own kind—to those in what he called their "bounded community." In other words, we apply the teaching of love only to those within our own sacred circles—fellow Christians, but not Muslims; fellow Muslims, but not Jews!

Unfortunately, those outside the sacred circle of our own bounded community too often are seen as other, alien, less than fully human. Sometimes they are seen as loathsome beasts. The love demand doesn't apply to them. In the words of a bit of popular doggerel, "Men drew a circle that shut me out, heretic, rebel, a thing to flout." Too often in the world's bloody history, people of faith have felt free—as in the case of last Tuesday—not only to reduce the outsider to less than human, but they also have felt compelled to hurt or destroy him.

So, who is God? The God of vengeance and holy war, or the heavenly Father of us all, who loves each as God loves all, and who loves all as God loves each. And who is my brother or sister?

Also crucial is how we understand what Isaiah calls the righteousness and salvation of God. The great twentieth-century American theologian, Reinhold Niebuhr, continually warned and worried about the tendency of every nation and every religious group to define their own truth as ultimate and final truth. (See especially his essays, "The Tower of Babel" and "The Test of True Prophecy" in his *Beyond Tragedy*.) We identify, he said, our own limited theology with the ultimate and absolute truth and our limited brand of justice with absolute justice. When we do that, we then turn a jaundiced eye on the beliefs and practices of others. We even go so far as to hold alien nations, religions, and cultures in contempt. From there it is only one short step to finding justification in the name of God and truth to do harm and even violence to the despised other.

Niebuhr goes so far as to insist every political establishment exists as a temporary compromise with some degree of injustice. What if that is true? What if every human order, whether in church or state, whether ours or another, is no more than partially just, no more than partially right and true? What if all our human institutions fall under the transcendent judgment of almighty God who, alone, is righteousness himself? That nothing is God but God and nothing is absolute, but the Absolute is one of the most important and profound of all religious insights. It is, in fact, the Protestant principle, and it is biblical! "As the heavens are high above the earth, so are my ways above your ways, says the Lord." Did not Paul conclude his hymn to love "Now we see through a glass darkly, but then face to face. Now we know in part, then shall we know as we are known" (1 Cor. 13:12)?

I recently overheard someone say he was tired and fed up with the theory of relativity, with the idea that everything was only relative—morals, values, social norms, and religious doctrines. I thought to myself, "Does he not understand? That mindset is what brought down the towers at the World Trade Center. It is the absolutist mindset—what I call the 100 percent mentality. It is the fanaticism of the true believer who has no patience for ambiguity, no truck with the unfinished and incomplete. He doesn't see through a glass darkly; he thinks he sees face to face. He doesn't know in part; he thinks he has the whole truth."

On our own part, shall we mirror the fanatics; insist with equal vigor on the complete justice of our own cause? What happens to humility in that picture? Like you, I find it painful to hear criticism of the things I treasure—my theology, point of view, politics, heroes, you name it. When Isaiah says that God and God's righteousness and salvation abide when all other foundations are swept away, he sets that solid foundation in contrast to all the perishing foundations we build—our most cherished beliefs and institutions. We deal here with the transcendence of God over against the finitude and limitations of the human. This essential understanding of what is eternal, including as it does the love of God and the brotherhood/sisterhood of all human beings, is what stands between us and the folly of fanaticism.

Considering times like this when the foundations are shaken, the theologian Paul Tillich turned to Psalm 102: "Thy years are throughout all generations of old. Thou hast laid the foundations of the Earth. The Heavens are the work of Thy hands. They vanish, but Thou shalt endure. They wear out like a robe. Thou changest them like garments. But Thou art the same and Thy years shall have no end." Tillich continued in his own words:

> When Earth grows old and wears out, when nations and cultures die, the Eternal changes the garment of His infinite being. He is the foundation on which all foundations are laid, and this foundation cannot be shaken. There is something immovable, unchangeable, unshakeable, eternal, which becomes evident in our passing and in the changing of our world. On the boundaries of the finite, the infinite becomes visible. In the light of the Eternal, the transitory-ness of the temporal appears.[2]

I think we see some of that with our own eyes today. After the towers came down, in the midst of the carnage, there was God. God was in the dust-caked and tear-streaked face of a New York fireman. I think I saw God also in all of those who in the best tradition of firefighting raced up the stairs, lugging their heavy gear, faces to the flames, while everyone else was rushing downstairs trying to escape. God is with us, I think, in the avalanche of compassion that has been released by this tragedy, for God and good are within us and between us as we reach out to each other. Thus we lit this morning the paschal candle to remind us of the presence of the Christ in the midst of chaos and that "nothing can separate us from the love of God which is in Christ Jesus our Lord."

Today's Old and New Testament texts link up just here. The abiding salvation and righteousness of God are synonymous with the love of God in Christ Jesus from which we cannot be separated, and that, in turn enables us to "be not anxious" as Paul enjoins in his Philippian letter. This is the perfect love that casts out fear and imparts that "peace that passes understanding" and "keeps our hearts in Christ Jesus." My associate in ministry put it unforgettably in a prayer last week: "Hate took love and buried it. Yet love was returned to us triumphant. Death took life and made away with it, but life rose again from the tomb. Evil slew holiness, yet holiness came back to life again."[3]

The Buddhists are right, of course. Their first law says life is sorrowful. Nor does the biblical witness promise God will put an invisible shield around us to fend off the "slings and arrows of outrageous fortune." Sooner or later, as Frederick Buechner once said, the worst happens to all of us. The bubble breaks. Our basic insecurity is revealed. The antidote to anxiety is not that we're perfectly protected. The antidote to anxiety is "nothing can separate us from the love of God in Christ Jesus our Lord."

With all this in mind, what is left to say? Perhaps one cautionary word. I never shall forget some words of my uncle Durward McCrary, an inveterate outdoorsman. The subject of rattlesnakes came up more than once on our hunting and fishing expeditions in West Texas. He told me, "Jimmy, always remember, the main thing about a rattlesnake is not what he can do to you. The main thing about a rattlesnake is what he can make you do to yourself!" The "rattlesnakes" we encounter today—the kind that blow up buildings and people—are dangerous indeed, lethally deadly, fanatically so. But they are not half so dangerous in what they can do to us as they are in what they can make us do to ourselves.

Notes

[1]John Donne, "Meditations from Devotions upon Emergent Occasions," XVII *Meditations, Seventeenth-Century Prose and Poetry*, ed. Coffin and Witherspoon (New York: Harcourt, Brace and Co, 1946), 68.

[2]Paul Tillich, "The Shaking of the Foundations," in *The Shaking of the Foundations* (New York: Charles Scribner's Sons, 1948), 9.

[3]Robert Dibble, unpublished prayer, River Road Church, Baptist.

(Dr. Slatton preached this sermon on the Sunday after the 9/11/2001 attacks.)

Jacob: God's Unlikely Choice

Genesis 27

(Spring 2008)

Have you noticed? In movies and novels, in history and in life, the rascals are the ones who rivet our attention? It is no different in the Bible. Even before he was born, Jacob seems to have been struggling for the upper hand. It was as if he were trying to beat out his twin brother in the race to be first out of his mother's womb. He was born "hanging on to his brother's heel"—as if to say, "Wait a minute brother! Let me go first." They named him Jacob, which, depending on how you parse it, means "he caught by the heel," or maybe "he kicks his way in or out with his heel." You even could render the name "the supplanter," which would suggest someone who keeps an eye out for the main chance, the kind of shark who ends up on K Street or at Goldman Sachs.

There was a prize at stake. It is called the law of primogeniture, which means the first-born son—the first male child—got everything when it came to inheritance—the whole herd, the whole farm, head of the family, the works. Today, that may sound antiquated and only mildly interesting. Then, it was the law of the land, the way the world was organized, and it made all the difference.

It was a way of protecting property, making sure a goodly inheritance did not get subdivided again and again, until after a few generations of that sort of dividing up the ancestral property, what was once a sizeable estate ended up being not a lot in the hands of one, but a little in the hands of many. (Even if you're not a fan of history, let me just add that in a lot of important places this went on for a very long time and was the way the great families held on to what they had, got more, and remained great over many generations.) It was also a way of avoiding disputes among beneficiaries. You couldn't very well sue your brother if the law clearly said the firstborn got it all. If you were a firstborn, it was a great system. If not—if you were not the son of promise—tough luck. You were a second-class citizen, dependent on your brother's charitable disposition.

All that was at stake was power. And it was, as I said, fair or foul, the way things were organized. To mess with primogeniture was to mess with the way the world was arranged. To challenge the system was to be a dangerous subversive. From the opening bell, it seems clear that the child born trying to pull his brother back and push himself forward was set against the way things were. If you think a fellow like Jacob will settle for the accident of birth order and meekly take his place at the foot of the table, guess again. If God's hand is anywhere in this, could it mean that he stands with the underdog—in this case the younger brother—or that he stands at odds with the way the world works?[1]

To add spice to the story, there was favoritism from the beginning. Esau, the heir apparent, by law the son of promise, was ruddy. He was born hairy, apparently with an abundance of testosterone. He was an outdoorsman, rugged, masculine, a man of the fields. Not surprisingly, he was his father's favorite. Jacob—"Heel"—on the other hand, was smooth, fairer skinned, stayed closer to home, and was his mother's son.

The theme plays out in a marvelous encounter between the two brothers. Jacob, the smooth one, the stay-at-home-with-women brother, is making some lentil soup. Esau comes in from the field starving. "Give me some of that red stew."

"Not so fast; you have to give me something in return."

"Like what?"

"Like your birthright."

"What use is a birthright to me if I perish from hunger now?" asks Esau. "All right, my, my birthright for your stew."

"Done!" declares Jacob. "But first you have to give me your solemn oath. Surrender your birthright to me here, now, today, and you can have this soup."

"I solemnly swear," says Esau.

"Here's the soup! Enjoy!" says Jacob.

God doesn't say anything at all, but God is more than watching. The writer, who generally shows Esau in a favorable light, says, "Esau showed by this how little he valued his birthright."

Remember, God's mission and God's blessing are what is at stake here. God's chosen instrument in the redemption of the world, his people, are here present in the person of the next heir to the promise, and we are watching that redemption enter and infuse a people.

As if the deal struck between the sons had never happened, certainly as if it had not changed things, Isaac, feeling his age, decides the time has come to begin passing the torch to his number-one son, Esau. So he tells Esau, "It is time for you to go on a hunt, find game, and make some of that savory stew that I love so well." It seems that more than one son knows how to cook. "We'll have a meal together, and I will give my fatherly blessing to you as the firstborn and son of promise."

Unluckily for Esau, his mother Rebecca overhears the conversation. After he sets out on his hunt, she tells Jacob what is afoot and offers a counter-plot. "Go to the herd, select two fine young goats. Bring them to me, and I'll make that savory stew your father likes so well, and you can take it to him and secure his blessing." Jacob, of course, is more than willing, but he is afraid the ruse will not work. "What if Dad sees through it? What if he recognizes me, and instead of blessing me, curses me?"

"Then the curse be on my head instead of yours," says Rebecca, making you think maybe this is a case of like mother, like son. So she makes that savory stew, and Jacob takes it to his father. But before he goes—you've got to love this—Rebecca gives Jacob Esau's clothes to wear, and she puts goat hide over his arms so they will feel like the arms of his hairy brother, and, on the back of his neck to boot.

"Who's there?" asks old Isaac when Jacob comes into his tent.

"It is I, your son Esau," lies Jacob. Just as he feared, his father is suspicious. "You got back from that hunt awfully fast. How did you make such a quick kill?"

"The Lord your God was with me, and put the beast right in my path," lies Jacob to his nearly blind old father.

Then the old man does a touching thing—no pun intended: He reaches out a hand to his lying son, and touches his arm. "Well, the hand is the hand of Esau," he says, more to himself than anyone else, "but the voice is the voice of Jacob." And the text says, "He blessed him." Still doubtful, the old man asks anyway, "Are you really my son Esau?"

"Yes, I am," says Jacob with sweet sincerity.

"Come near my son, and kiss me."

So Jacob embraces his father and kisses him. And Isaac, taking in the odors of Esau's hunting clothes and of the goatskin, says, "Bless the Lord, I smell my son, and it is like the smell of the open country." Convinced, old Isaac pronounces his solemn blessing, not on his firstborn, but upon the younger twin:

> God give you dew from heaven
> And the richness of the earth,
> Corn and new wine in plenty.
> May peoples serve you
> And nations bow down to you.
> May you be lord over your brothers,
> And may your mother's sons bow down to you.
> A curse on those who curse you. (Gen. 27:27-29)

No sooner has Jacob left with this new confirmation that the birthright and the role of son of promise are his by his clever hustling, than Esau enters his father's tent with a fresh and savory game stew. Father and son are appalled, and Esau says, "This is the second time that 'Heel' has supplanted me. First he swindled me out of my birthright; now he has stolen my blessing. My father's getting older. As long as that old man lives, Jacob lives, because I will not bring down on my father—does this remind you of anything? —the grief of one son murdering another, but as soon as he is gone, then I'm going to kill my brother Jacob."

Secrets like that are not easily kept in a family. Rebecca warns Jacob that his brother is planning to kill him and tells him he must flee for his life. In fact, she sends him back to the place where her husband Isaac found her: far and away from the tents of Isaac, back to her own home and family. She sends him to the protection of her brother Laban.

Away from family and home, a fugitive from his brother's anger and alone, Jacob comes to a place in the open country where he can find nothing softer than a stone on the ground under the open sky for a pillow and bed. But while he sleeps he has an amazing dream. It is the first time in the text when the God of Abraham and Isaac, the God whose inscrutable will is somehow at work in this tangled tale, speaks in the story of "Heel."

In a dream that is more like a vision, Jacob sees a sort of ramp, or stairway to the stars. My translation calls it what long tradition has called it: a ladder connecting earth and heaven—I like ramp better. The angels, the messengers of God are going and coming on the errands to which God sends them. More than that, Jacob hears God speaking:

> I am the Lord, the God of Abraham your grandfather, and Isaac your father. The land on which you lie now, I am going to give to you and to your descendants after you. These descendants of yours will be as numerous as the grains of dust beneath your feet. They will spread far and wide. All the families of earth will want to be blessed as you and your descendants are blessed. I will go with you, protect you, and bring you safely home, and I will not leave you until I've done what I've promised you. (Gen. 28:13-15)

And Jacob says, "The Lord is in this place, and I did not know it. Surely this is the house of God. This is the gate to heaven."

Maybe we should pause here. Would the point be that anywhere we find ourselves is an intersection between heaven and earth, between God and us? Jesus said the kingdom of God is as close as your next breath.

Jacob sets up the stone on which he had slept as a memorial, pours oil on it as a sign of dedication, naming the place Beth-El, which means "house of God." He follows all this amazing experience and act of worship and dedication by making a vow. Unfortunately, I have to tell you his vow sounds like a contract—the sort of contract a shrewd fellow would concoct. "If," he says, "God will protect me, see that I have food and clothes and a roof over my head and safety, and bring me back home in one piece, then God can be my God. Then this stone will be a house of God and I'll give God a tenth of everything I get" (Gen. 28:20-22). And God is at work through this fellow? How can God bear to lower himself to work with such a selfish person, and how can God not be insulted by that reference to building God a shrine and giving God a cut of ten percent in return for all God is promising to do for Jacob and his descendants? What possibly can come of a relationship that begins in this fashion? Is there something here we are missing?

Laban, of course, was Rebecca's brother and Jacob's uncle. Blood seems to be thicker than water, as they say. What went on between uncle and nephew from that point on proved to be astounding—the deals they struck, the maneuvers they made to get the better of one another. Jacob said he was so taken with Laban's younger daughter (again the younger instead of the firstborn) that he would work seven years for her. The deal was struck, and Jacob was as good as his word, but not Laban.

At the end of the seven years the wedding was held, the bride went to the tent of the groom, but the next morning, the bride turned out to be not Rachel, whom Jacob loved and had worked seven years to win, but her older and plainer sister Leah. The trickster tricked! The con artist conned! It is enough to make you weep with laughter. Not for nothing did Middle Eastern women wear those veils and burkas. When Jacob demanded an explanation, Laban said, "Well, in this country and in this age, it is not customary for the younger sister to marry until the older sister is married. But, if you insist you can have Rachel too, only you'll have to work another seven years for her." So smitten was Jacob, and such an operator, he agreed to the deal and spent the next seven years working for his uncle and father-in-law in return for the privilege of marrying Rachel.

After that, Jacob worked another six years during which he managed to gain possession of the greater and healthier part of his father-in-law's livestock. When he had completely worn out his welcome, he collected his goats, sheep, camels, cattle, his two wife-cousins—Leah and Rachel—their two handmaidens (who had somehow become his surrogate wives and the mothers of four of his children), his eleven sons by these four women, and, thanks to Rachel, even the household gods of his pagan uncle and rode as swiftly away as he could with all of that loot and all those herds and herdsmen. In short, he had become the father of a tribe and a very wealthy man in his own right, but not someone who bore any resemblance to God's last, best hope for humanity.

There was a subsequent meeting and truce to be made with Laban, and that done, Jacob was on his homeward way. All that remained was to face the brother he had wronged twenty years before, Esau, who, at that very moment was riding toward him at the head of four hundred men. Before the two brothers meet again, however, Jacob will be assailed by an even more imposing adversary in a meeting that will leave him forever limping and with a new name. Stay tuned.

Note

[1] Walter Brueggemann, *Genesis* (Atlanta: John Knox Press, 1982), 210.

The Gift

Luke 2:1-12

(December 19, 1999)

"While they were there, the time came for her baby to be born, and she gave birth to a son, her firstborn. She wrapped him in swaddling clothes and laid him in a manger, because there was no room for them in the house."

Sometime back, a story was going around that, for me, is a perfect parable for Christmas. Whether the story was true or an "urban legend" or a work of fiction, I cannot say. As best as I can reconstruct it from memory, it goes like this:

A rather disreputable-looking fellow showed up at a big-steeple church and asked for the pastor. One look at the man convinced the receptionist that the pastor probably should be shielded from such a person, especially one who just walked in off the street. But the rumpled and not-too-cleanly-shaven stranger insisted. He had a package to deliver, he said, and his instructions were to hand it to the pastor in person. There were whispered consultations between secretaries, and furtive side glances at the stranger. But as he would neither take no for an answer nor volunteer to depart the premises, the pastor duly received him. The stranger held out a fat and somewhat soiled envelope. The minister took it with some reluctance. "What is this?" "I don't know. You will have to see for yourself." "Who is it from?" "The person who sent it didn't say; just asked me to deliver it to you in person. That's all I know," said the messenger, and with that he was gone.

This rather strange meeting took place at a time when letter bombs were in the news. The package looked as if it might qualify—a large, fat, sealed, and soiled envelope. There was nothing about the stranger to herald the usual deliveryman. Neither his appearance nor the manner of his coming and going had inspired confidence or betokened reliability. He looked like the sort of fellow who shouldn't be left by himself in the front office. The minister actually considered soaking the package in a bucket of water, or calling the police to check it out. But, at last, he decided to open it. Inside the package were $11,000 in currency, sent by someone who wished to make an anonymous donation to the church!

The Christmas story is strikingly similar. Once upon a time, God tried to give the world an incredibly valuable gift. Amazingly he had a hard time getting the intended recipients to accept. The innkeeper said, "Put it in the stable." Herod said, "The best thing to do with him is to kill him before he has a chance to grow up and cause trouble." Even Joseph said, "I think I will break the engagement quietly so as not to cause the poor girl too much embarrassment." Christmas is about a gift that was not so easy to give, a gift that we are still reluctant to receive. No, better, a gift we affect to receive, but maybe never really expect to open. We are much too polite to refuse the gift. We graciously accept the package, offer heartfelt thanks, go through with the celebration, but leave the gift in the wrapper without ever fully unpacking it.

The fact is that we are not so sure about the gift. We are not sure it is a gift at all. Even if it is free, we are not sure we want the full contents. How are we to be certain that if we accept the package it won't turn out to be something of a letter bomb?

One of our problems is that life is the medium in which the gift of God is given and in which it must be received. That's what the feed box, the swaddling clothes, and that celebrated manger are all about. Christ was given to Mary in the form of an awkward pregnancy, an infant son, and an arduous journey to pay taxes. It is not hard to imagine her answering, "I don't want to be in this play."

Monday morning comes, ready or not. Life knocks at the door like a disreputable stranger. You open the door, and there is an unwanted illness or a mess to clean up or a lifetime of hard work—mouths to feed, demands to be met, calls to answer. It is all a mixed bag, looking for all the world like a dirty envelope, delivered by a not-too-solid-looking stranger, and containing God knows what. Who's to blame you if you don't wish to accept delivery?

The risk, of course, is not only that one might reject the whole gift of life completely and out of hand. Too many do! A recent survey found that fully a fourth of high school students interviewed had seriously considered suicide. Still there are other less direct but quite effective ways of returning God's gift of life unopened to the sender. One way is to fail to plumb the negatives—troubles, disappointments, hardships, and losses. They can kill you, of course. But when they don't, they are often the bearers of concealed blessings. As the saying goes, "Things that don't kill you outright can make you stronger."

By the Jabbok, with Esau riding against him with four hundred armed men, Jacob was beset by a mysterious presence, and wrestled with him all night. Wisely, he said to his adversary, "I will not turn you loose until you bless me." Ever afterwards he limped. But he emerged from the struggle with a new name and a blessing. To seize the hard questions, to wrestle with them 'til dawn, refusing to let them go until they tell us their real names and even give their blessing is the wisdom of the Jacob story. Unfortunately, we are too often like Lucy in the "Peanuts" cartoon: We want "ups, ups, ups, all ups, no downs." If there is suffering that ought to be avoided, there is also suffering that must be accepted and endured. If Mary had refused the journey, hard as it was, if she had disdained or discounted the stuff of her own experience, would she not have denied also the gift of God that was given within the fabric of her own life?

The gift Christmas offers us is not just the birth of the Christ in Bethlehem of Judea, in the days of Herod the king, when Quirinius was governor of Syria. The promise and point of it all is the birth of the Christ in you. He is to be re-presented, enfleshed in you, to take form in your life. Or, to put it in bolder terms, you are supposed to become a son or daughter of God yourself. In the words of Samuel Miller, "We are born into the world and all our living after that is the struggle to be born into the spirit."[1] This birth into the spirit is the destiny God intends by giving us existence.

There are many metaphors in Scripture for the reality of Christ coming to birth in and through us. It is life, as opposed to merely living, having one's eyes opened, receiving the gift of hearing. It is being awakened, raised from the dead. In the language of the church, it is conversion. In the imagery of Jesus, it is to be born again. However pictured, this is the single and essential task for each of us.[2]

The struggle to be born into the spirit is a life-long task, requiring not one conversion but many, for there are many levels of the soul, many sides to a person's life. Not only the mind needs conversion, but also the emotions. The imagination needs transformation as well as the will.

In his autobiographical *War as I Knew It*, George Patton warned of the military error of stopping, as he put it, on the wrong side of a river. The idea was that when an army reached a barrier or objective such as a river, that barrier should be crossed and defenses thrown up on the far side.

The same is true in the life of the spirit. Too many people assume that conversion has only to do with the beginning of faith. They only get their feet wet. They never go all out. If there is only one conversion in Christian experience, why did Jesus say to Simon Peter long after he was a disciple, "When you are converted, strengthen your brethren" (Luke 22:32)? Antoine de Saint-Exupery was right. There may be sudden illuminations, dramatic and seemingly instantaneous transformations, but they are always granted at the end of a long and gradual preparation.

One thing is certain: One cannot borrow a ready-to-wear soul. There is no place for proxy faith. David cannot wear the armor of Saul. Here is the most subtle and devastating way of spurning the gift of God: to discount the experience and struggle of one's own soul.

In Ibsen's play, Peer Gynt is a sort of Scandinavian Everyman. One day on the way to a funeral he chances to meet at a crossroads a strange character called the Button Moulder. The Button Moulder informs him that he is seeking Peer Gynt. It seems that Peer's own coffin is ready, his grave dug, and the day at hand for the settlement of accounts. Peer is a person of whom it is said that he is like an onion—many layers, no core. The Button Moulder tells him that he was intended to be "a bright and shiny button on the world's waistcoat." In the strange and compelling imagery of the story, Peer is told that his body will return to the earth, but his soul like a faulty metal button is to be put back into the Master's melting ladle and to be melted down. When he protests that he is no great sinner, the Button Moulder replies that is just the point: "There is no need for you to make so great a fuss about so small a thing; because you have never been yourself. What difference can it make to you if, when you die, you disappear?"[3]

Like Peer Gynt, some of us fail to make the journey for ourselves. As Samuel Miller has said, we dress our souls in the piety of others, as if we were spiritual paupers who must wear hand-me-downs. We do not make our own prayers, or even repent of our own sins.[4] We feel we must conform to the prescribed opinions of others. We are as full of opinions as a monkey is of fleas, and to no better purpose. Someone once said of the poet Robert Frost, "He made up in opinions what he lacked in ideas."[5] It is possible to become a private collection of public opinions. We need to ask our own questions, own our doubts, and let our souls speak for themselves. Perhaps the most suspicious-looking envelope that is delivered to one's door is one's own soul, and the messenger none other than your own slice of experience and reality. More than one has slammed the door in the face of that messenger.

The promise of Christmas is that the gift will be offered. That is the great good news. You can count on the offer coming to your door, wrapped in the swaddling clothes of everyday events, laid in the feed box of your common life, showing up in the cattle shed of the ordinary. Always the gift is gently offered, not forced. No bullying is allowed. The divine giver himself insists upon your freedom. He makes himself and his gifts vulnerable to voluntary acceptance or rejection. This is the heart of the priesthood of each individual before the mystery of divine self-giving.

In his writings championing religious freedom and the separation of church and state, Roger Williams reasoned that freedom from compulsion and constraint was necessary as the condition of authentic religious decision. He did not make freedom an end in itself. He saw it as the necessary oxygen in which the soul could live and breathe.

To change the imagery only slightly, the gift of the kingdom comes like an invitation to a banquet. No one can go for you. No one else can accept in your behalf. You must be your own priest because it is within the fabric of your own life in the world that the gift is given, the invitation to the banquet of the kingdom issued. The flash of recognition, the "aha" reaction, must be your own. Nor for that matter can you recognize the kingdom and enter into it for another. The best you can do is to point to the places where the kingdom appears, to bear witness to its reality.

Once upon a time, God determined to give to us a very great and precious gift. The gift came wrapped in the whole package of life, and as someone has said, "Trouble is the only flavor in which life comes." The gift was given in the person of the Christ with the intention that he take flesh and form in us, and that looked like a painful and disturbing proposition. The gift, moreover, was offered in and through the experiences and hungers, the struggles and anguish of our own souls. Wrapped as it was in the unexpected, delivered in such unorthodox fashion, we were tempted not to receive shipment. Christmas is about a gift God tries to give.

Notes

[1] Samuel H. Miller, *The Great Realities* (New York: Harper & Brothers, 1955), 33.

[2] Ibid., 22.

[3] Henrik Ibsen, Peer Gynt, Act V, Scene 7 in Eleven Plays of Henrik Ibsen, *The Modern Library* (Random House), 166-67.

[4] Samuel H. Miller, *The Life of the Soul* (New York: Harper & Row, 1951), 21.

[5] W. B. J. Martin, "Going All the Way," unpublished sermon preached in Dallas (November 15, 1965).

The Resurrection—After Easter

John 21:1-17; 1 Corinthians 15:3-11

(May 6, 1984)

Today is the third Sunday of Easter. Two weeks ago in a sanctuary overflowing with members and visitors, we thrilled to the proclamation that Christ was raised from the dead. Buoyed by the grandeur of the words and the music and the moment, our spirits resonated to the reality of a living Lord. But then, Easter Sunday came and went, and so did the crowds and the orchestra. Now, although the lectionary calls for a third Sunday of teaching and preaching on the Easter theme, this present moment is feeling more and more like ordinary time. Dare we admit, for most of us, the excitement has waned? If the excitement wears off, the crowds go home—as they most always do—and there are no more trumpets, what then? Is anything really any different than before?

Our gospel lesson for this Sunday from the twenty-first chapter of John's Gospel speaks exactly to that question. For the disciples, as for us, Easter has come and gone. John shifts the scene from Jerusalem to the Galilee. The disciples—at least some of them—have gone home, back to their old haunts. I think John intends for us to understand that means back to ordinary life. The unspoken question, of course, is how the resurrection of Jesus affects the real world to which the disciples must return and within which they must live. In a few spare sentences the Gospel makes us almost painfully aware of the ordinariness, the everydayness, the unchanged sameness, of the world to which the disciples have returned.

After a time Simon Peter says, "I don't know about the rest of you, but I'm going fishing." The others—I imagine somewhat aimlessly and without much enthusiasm—decide to go with him. They fish all night and come up empty-handed. I would bet they have been in that situation many a time before. Does John mean to use their empty nets and fruitless toil as an image of stubborn reality, unbent, unchanged, and unyielding, no matter what happened at that tomb or in that garden in Jerusalem? Maybe it is just me, but I cannot escape a certain feeling for the whole scene that early morning by the lakeside. Do you sense it too? Did they? Was there a sense of emptiness, an impression of anticlimax? Did their universe seem alien and indifferent?

In my mind's eye I see a great yawning sky, the silent arid hills framing the lake, and I seem to hear the soft rhythm of the waves lapping the shore. I wonder if to them, as to me, life had settled back to business as usual. Did they know then, empty-handed and muscle-sore, that resurrection or no resurrection, life went on, and the world to all appearances went blindly on as before? Were they troubled by the thought that all of the powers of earth, all the principalities of their world were back in business at the same old stands and the same old prices: the haggling still going on in the market place, the conniving in the palace? Is that what their tired eyes told them; that despite what they had seen in Jerusalem, the cruel old world just kept rolling along?

I well remember my own impression on first visiting the Holy Land—what seemed to me at the time a great and ironic emptiness. Nowhere did I discern remarkable transformation, nowhere any sign that Messiah had come and his reign begun. In the city of Jerusalem there were bullet holes in so many walls. At the Hadassah Hospital they showed us Chagall's famous stained glass windows depicting images of Israel's history. In one of them there was a hole where a shell fragment had torn through.

> After two thousand years of mass,
> We've got as far as poison-gas.
>
> —Thomas Hardy
> "Christmas: 1924"

In Lebanon, there was anarchy. In Jerusalem, there was the atmosphere of "fortress Israel" On the street you were likely to see a pretty young woman strolling during an afternoon with an automatic weapon slung over her shoulder as casually as if it were her purse. The random explosion of a hidden bomb somewhere in the country was an almost common occurrence. In Nazareth, coming out of a church, I saw a priest break up a fist fight between a man and his smaller, younger brother. The contradiction was palpable—is palpable—not only there, of course, but in the rest of our world as well.

The Jews, considering the deplorable state of things, say, "When the Messiah comes, things will be different." We Christians say, despite the deplorable state of things, say, "Nevertheless, the Messiah has come." He came two thousand years ago, the Prince of Peace, the Messiah, the Savior of the world. We proclaim that the crucified Jesus was raised by God from the dead on Easter, and his triumph was secured. Yet our world remains distressingly the same.

The disciples themselves are back at what we might call business as usual, at the same old place, back where they started. Well, where else should they be? After a while, what is there to do but to go back home, to your livelihood, to the world of passing events. You can't run at fever pitch or on enthusiasm all the time. So how does resurrection work after Easter?

Here is our first clue: just here in the text and in the middle of an utterly ordinary morning! Suddenly they encounter Jesus. In their weariness and defeat, surrounded by boats and empty nets, just at dawn, and quite unexpectedly, they run up against . . . him! Is it too much of a stretch for us to hear John saying the living Lord is found within the day-to-day events of ordinary life—like fishing all night and catching nothing—or, perhaps, in making one last try on the other side of the boat? Maybe he even means to say Messiah is to be encountered in the other, as, for instance, in that strangely mysterious and solitary figure hailing them from shore: "Boys, have you caught anything?"

Look closely. The disciples are discovering the Christ who stands within every situation and between them and all they encounter. What they find at the lake is that the crucified Jesus has been raised up to be the eternal contemporary, the one who is always there. They are learning they cannot go home or anywhere else without him. They are learning what we also have learned, that the Jesus crucified at Calvary has been raised by God, and he stands forever, not only with God but also with us as our constant hope (Savior) and inescapable Lord and guide. Asking nothing for himself, living in poverty, dying in defeat and disgrace, he so commands our consciences and souls we cannot forget him. We cannot expunge him from our innermost thoughts. That is what became evident that day at what John calls the sea (read, lake) of Tiberius.

Ever since, people have known nothing better to do with what is broken and warped and evil than to hold it out to him with a cry for healing, restitution, and forgiveness. Ever since, people have known nothing better to do with their dying than to do it with prayers to him on their lips. Countless numbers of us have shaped our dying prayers with Jesus' own words from the cross, "Father, into your hands I commend my spirit." Ever since, we have known nothing better to do with our hopes, aspirations, and possibilities than to bring them to him and make the great petition, "Lord have mercy, Christ have mercy, Lord have mercy."

Not only does Jesus make his living presence known at the lake, but he also appears as the *constant mediator*, as the one who literally stands between his followers and all else, including their own souls. By mediator I mean he ever insists on defining and reshaping all their relationships—to things, to others, to life, to God, and to themselves. This is the "take away" from the appearance of Jesus at the lake, not only for his disciples, but also for us.

Just as he stood between the fisherman and their nets, boats, fishing, and surroundings, he stands between us and our stuff. We can no longer treat the world of things, even our dearest possessions, as if we answer for them to no one but ourselves. We are, as he taught his first followers, stewards of a world that belongs only to him. We cannot treat our own selves without his interference, without seeing ourselves in the light of Christ. As the Apostle put it, we are not "our own," we are "bought with a price." Paul spoke of himself as a slave of Jesus Christ.

Nor can we deal immediately and uninterrupted with others, not even our own kith and kin. Even our very own parents, children, wives, husbands, uncles and aunts, cousins, and in-laws must be treated as Christ would have us treat them. He gets between us. That is what "mediator" means. He stands as the eternal contemporary, the ever-present one between us and them, and would shape the relationship according to his nature and purpose. Indeed, if we are properly sensible of him, we find it impossible to look at a single soul without seeing that one as bearing the image of Christ—no matter how lowly or how debased that person may seem. As the disciples found Jesus present at the lakeshore, we find him, if we pay attention, in the last and least, and especially in those who need us.

Note well: As real and true to character as the appearance of Jesus was, there was also a whole new indefinable dimension to this risen one. John calls that figure at the lakeshore Jesus. John says they all recognized him. But, John also says that no one dared ask the one question on the tip of everyone's tongue. John tells us what that question was: "Who are you?" Strange! What are we to make of this? John leaves no question about the reality of the resurrection, but he also makes clear there is something about this new reality that exceeds our grasp, much less our comprehension. As real and vital as the risen Jesus appears in John's text, as down to earth and human as that exchange beside the boats, it is clear that neither they nor we can own it, nor can place ourselves in command of it.

We Westerners, of course, prefer stuff we can manage. We are technocrats who have grown comfortable with mechanisms that put the forces of nature to work at our disposal. Flip the light switch, and the power is there. So much do we depend on the predictable that, when, say, your automobile breaks down, it can ruin your week. How is it possible that mechanical beast is not faithfully available at your every whim? We like what we can comprehend, and if not comprehend, then at least manage and control.

Our story of Jesus' appearance by the lake makes clear we are confronted by a different kind of reality altogether. To themselves, the disciples said of what they saw, "It is Jesus." But no mother's son among them could muster the effrontery to ask him to his face, "Who are you?" The mind sticks on that, does it not? Do you find yourself wondering, as I do, whether one of them might have said, "Oh, that's Aaron, Simon's second cousin? He's come down here this morning to buy some fish?" Might the whole incident have been passed off as a meeting with a stranger that proved uncannily evocative of Jesus? In fact, we are left not only with a sense of the transcendent, of the mysterious, but we are also left with the freedom to take the whole thing one way or the other. After all, as a wise man once said, if there is no room for doubt, there is no room for our freedom. In fact, if there is no room for doubt, there is no room for faith. As Carlyle Marney taught, "Doubt is faith's backside."

Life does seem in so many ways to be just as it always has been, as I discovered in Jerusalem, and as you have discovered wherever you've been. That, of course, is how the faith has always been. Christ's resurrection is the first fruit of a victory already won and yet to be won. There is an already and a not-yet quality to the kingdom of God as proclaimed by Jesus and as vindicated and sealed in God's raising him from the dead. That Christ lives forever as both our Savior and Lord, however convincingly presented in gospel and sermon, remains a possibility accessible only to faith. I can live into resurrection or not. It is entirely up to me. It is completely up to you. Take the gamble, or not.

We must not forget that the one who was raised from the dead, the one revealed to the disciples at the lake in the Galilee was Jesus—the lowly and self-emptying Jesus of poverty, weakness, servanthood, and compassion. Ever since, the best thing people have known to say about God is that he is like Jesus, and the most ultimately true thing anyone can say about what it means to be human in the best sense of the word is to be like Jesus. It was Jesus who was raised. The greatest possibility and the greatest curse of the Christian movement is that it is full of people who love Jesus, but do not love what Jesus is all about. If you wish to participate in resurrection, you must invest yourself in the way of Jesus, in what Jesus was and is about. (See the whole story of the four Gospels, with special attention to the Sermon on the Mount.)

Finally, what our text tells us is that it was the crucified Jesus who was raised from the dead. Resurrection never occurs anywhere except after a crucifixion, after a death. But I don't want to be "crucified with Christ," and I certainly don't want to die. Yet, that is the only way to be "raised up." I believe to catch the full meaning of this and not to do too much violence to our text, we need to expand our definition of dying to include what some have called "all the little deaths." By this is meant the many little deaths of denying the self-centered self, of following after the self-giving Jesus.

Jesus taught that the one who seeks to save his life will surely lose it, but I am still busy trying my best to save my own life. Jesus taught, "He who exalts himself will be abased." I take that to mean only the one who braves the little death of self-abasement, the lowly way of the servant, will be raised up. I still seek to exalt myself. Jesus said, only he who takes up his cross and follows him will be raised up. We do our best to avoid getting hurt. We do not want the little death, not even the little death of owning our guilt and making the prayer of brutally honest and thorough confession of our real sins. We don't like the little death of failure. We don't like the little death of suffering. No one in his right mind does. No one seeks out these things.

Can it be, however, that we would not so much fear death itself if we could bring ourselves first to undergo these little deaths encompassed in following the crucified? Could it be we would not fear death or the little deaths so much if we could fully appreciate the wisdom that "except a grain of wheat fall into the ground and die it abideth alone"? Resurrection follows a lifetime of dying to self in service and obedience, of taking the grand risk that on the other side of that dying there is resurrection, an empty grave, and a grand reunion.

The meeting by the lakeshore in Galilee makes clear that the resurrection was rather mysterious, not entirely comprehensible, and certainly not manageable. That is because resurrection catches us by surprise, as if out of nowhere, and it is always what happens from God's side when we've reached the end of our tethers, exhausted our human best. Since that is an extremity we tend to avoid, we don't often encounter resurrection.

By the way, it is well to remember that resurrection is always accessible only to the eye of faith. Jesus appeared by the lake to his friends, not his enemies. What John has given us in this third appearance of Jesus to his disciples is a picture of the earliest church trying to begin living with resurrection—after Easter. On this gloomy, rainy Sunday morning, with half the Easter crowd missing and no brass, that's our task as well.

Overtaken by Easter

Luke 24:13-35

(March 30, 1997)

I have a young friend who doesn't come to Easter services anymore. He finds them difficult because he doesn't believe in resurrection.

It's not easy, you know. How many of you have run into resurrection lately? Oh, we come to church on a day like this, glorious in spring. The trumpets are magnificent. The music lifts us, and for a moment we almost believe. We hope it is so. We hope Jesus once rose from the dead and the blessed in the Lord will escape the grip of death. But, it isn't easy to believe in resurrection. Sometimes we go away with the sense that the whole Easter promenade was a bit unreal—fragile, yes, beautiful, yes—but unreal.

I think the disciples would understand that, don't you? That's why one of my favorite stories is the one that Luke tells in chapter 24 of his gospel. Here are his words from the New English Bible:

"That same day two of them were on their way to a village called Emmaus, about seven miles from Jerusalem, talking together about all that had happened. As they talked and argued, Jesus himself came up and walked along with them."

(He often does, you know.)

But something kept them from recognizing who he was.

(It often does, you know.)

He asked them, "What is it you are debating as you walk?" They halted. Their faces full of gloom, and one of them called Cleopas answered, "Are you the only person staying in Jerusalem not to know what has happened there in the last few days?" "What do you mean?" he said. "All this about Jesus of Nazareth," they replied. "A prophet powerful in speech and action before God and the whole people; how our chief priests and rulers handed him over to be sentenced to death and crucified him. But we had been hoping that he was the man to liberate Israel."

(We have been hoping, too. Sometimes our hopes are dashed also. So we know where they were on the road. They were living the death of hope.)

"What is more, this is the third day since it happened, and now some women of our company have astounded us. They went early to the tomb, but failed to find his body and returned with a story that they had seen a vision of angels that told them he was alive. So some of our people went to the tomb and found things just as the women had said; but him they did not see."

(Some Bible scholars think this is an interpolation, that these men did not have knowledge of the report that the tomb was empty, but that Luke has worked in this reference to the empty tomb story to provide dramatic background.)

"But him they did not see."

(As we make our way along a familiar road with our own hopes dashed, we too have heard reports of a resurrection—back there, then, over yonder—but not here.)

"How dull you are!" he answered. "How slow to believe all that the prophets said! Was the Messiah not bound to suffer thus before entering upon his glory?" Then he began with Moses and all the prophets and explained to them the passages that referred to him in every part of the Scriptures.

By this time they had reached the village, to which they were going, and he made as if to continue his journey, but they pressed him: "Stay with us, for evening is drawing on, and the day is almost over." So he went in to stay with them. And when he had sat down with them at table, he took bread and said the blessing: he broke bread, and offered it to them. Then their eyes were opened, and they recognized him; and he vanished from their sight. They said to one another, "Did we not feel our hearts on fire as he talked with us on the road and explained the Scriptures to us?"

Where do you look for resurrection? And how do you recognize resurrection when you encounter it? That is the question and the thrust of this text.

I imagine those two fellows must have been feeling rather foolish as well as sad. After all, it must have seemed to them as they trudged along the road that the whole Jesus adventure had proved a forlorn hope. How had they allowed themselves to get so caught up in it all to leave hearth and home to follow him?

What possessed them to imagine that they, of all people, would be the ones to first meet and recognize the Messiah when he arrived to establish his kingdom? They had allowed themselves to be completely carried away.

But then he went up against the Jerusalem crowd, and he hit the realities of Jerusalem with all the impact of a light bulb on a concrete floor. Oh, they made hash of him, the powers that be, unceremoniously and quite effectively. When they had had enough of his antics—cleansing the temple, driving out the money changers, defying their customs—they didn't even have a sense of humor about it. They dragged him before the Roman procurator and then before their puppet king Herod. They raked him over the coals, stripped him, beat him, and humiliated him. When they were finished they had what was left of him taken out and nailed up to die. Cynically they nailed up over his head a sign that read, "This is the Jew King," and that, as they say, was that. Game, set, and match. Or, as Flannery O'Connor put it, you can't be any poorer than dead.

On the way . . .

Three days later, two dispirited followers were on their way home nursing their disappointment. I'm convinced Luke has given us their story not only as a confirmation that God wouldn't settle for the defeat of the cross, but also to give us a virtual template of how to recognize the reality and power of the resurrection when and where we encounter it.

I am impressed that for the two on the Emmaus road, the new reality found them while they were on the way. Maybe Emmaus was home, and that is where you go when there seems nowhere else to go. Maybe they had friends there. They were headed into whatever future remained for them. They were headed back to the real world and ordinary human life—the mixed bag of actual living, the ambiguous, the unexceptional, the nitty-gritty—what Emily Dickinson meant by "tomorrow, on this little street, in this little house." In other words they were on their way to where one least expects to encounter the divine, much less a resurrection.

Maybe this is what Jesus meant when he said, "Go tell Peter and the disciples, 'I go before you into Galilee.'" Why Galilee? Because that is where they lived. In other words, they were headed into space the risen Lord insists on claiming—the future, the whole world out there, ordinary human existence—life! It is the last place they—or we—expect to run into him; it is the first place he shows up.

After a crucifixion . . .

Of course, what overhangs their journey is the crucifixion of Jesus—the obscene contradiction of everything he was and stood for.

A Sunday school teacher asked his class of adolescent children what one must do to be forgiven. One of the boys answered, "You have to sin." It was not the expected answer, but it was a true answer nonetheless. In like manner for there to be a resurrection, there must be first a death—a crucifixion.

Without realizing it, the fellows on the Emmaus road were in the right place for resurrection. Having followed the Master, suffered the execution of hope, the contradiction of their faith in the reign of the Messiah, and the crucifixion of the one who embodied that hope and reign, they were in the valley of the shadow of death. They were in brokenness, grief, and despair. Without realizing it, they were in exactly the right place for resurrection.

I recall a story I heard Carlyle Marney tell on himself. He was in conversation with Albert Outler, the fine Methodist theologian who taught at Southern Methodist University in Dallas. Marney said he confided to Outler that it was hard to believe in the resurrection, and at times he found he was unable to do so. As I remember the story, Marney quoted Outler as replying, "Marney, don't you know you are not supposed to believe in the resurrection all the time?" Marney said, "Albert, you're so (expletive deleted) smart, when am I supposed to believe it?" And Outler said, "When you die, or when someone you love dies."

Another Marney story in circulation goes to the same point. In one of his many lecture and sermon appearances on college campuses, he was asked by students to talk about the resurrection. To make a point and tease their interest no doubt, he is reported to have refused. He said he didn't talk to people like them about resurrection. They were, he said, too healthy, too young, too full of hope and promise, and, all in all, at too much of an advantage to understand resurrection. They would need to grow older and suffer first.

It is the nature of this reality we call resurrection that it is the sort of life that comes out of death, a light that emerges out of darkness, the remarkable rise of good out of evil. This is what we celebrate when we arrange ourselves every Sunday in cruciform, literally in a room shaped like a cross. The long center aisle stretching from narthex straight through the chancel to the *reredos* is the vertical beam. The cross-aisle or transept aisle is the horizontal beam of the cross. The center aisle carries the gaze forward to the table where we place the bread and wine representative of the broken body and shed blood. Behind the table stands the *reredos* and upon it the cross to which the center aisle draws our attention. The cruciform life of death to the self-centered self and of self-forgetful love and service to which Jesus consistently invites his followers puts us into a way the world will punish and crucify. But it is the crucified who was raised and who is the beneficiary of the reality of resurrection.

It was Jesus who was raised to God and glory . . .

Of course, resurrection is not just a matter of God bringing life out of death. The point is which life. As any horror movie demonstrates, the mere survival of death is not necessarily good news. Who wants a revivified Frankenstein or one of the real Frankenstein monsters of history such as Hitler or Stalin? It was Jesus the self-emptying servant of God who was denied, rejected, and crucified. It was his teaching and way that was spurned and defeated in his death. In raising him, God reversed the judgment of the world and vindicated Jesus and the Christ life he so perfectly personified and embodied. Resurrection is the survival and ultimate triumph of Jesus' unique kind of good, of what he called the Kingdom of God.

If you seek a sign of resurrection, look no further than signs of the survival and durability of the Jesus way. We've never gotten completely past or away from his words or way, have we? Hardly. Not at all. However unrealistic and impractical his counsels may seem, however often we try life a different way, we cannot quite rid ourselves of the nagging sense that we should be doing what he said: going the second mile, turning the other cheek, forgiving seventy-times seven, praying for our enemies, standing up to the worst for the sake of the last and least. Have you managed entirely to get away from all that?

Have you noticed how he and his way keep coming back up out of the grave and surviving everything that history can do to efface and destroy them? I do not know how much faith you came with this morning, but think of this. Not many of us here today would wish to die without calling for the presence and assistance of the carpenter who got himself killed two thousand years ago. I wouldn't wish to do so, would you? Likewise, I doubt many of us are free of the haunting power of an invitation first uttered long ago, but still echoing in the deepest chambers of our consciousness, "Take up your cross and follow me." How's that for resurrection? How is that for "immortality"?

It is amazing that Jesus got out of his grave. It is stunning he came back after being hung up, stabbed with a spear, perforated with nails, pilloried in the glaring heat of the Judean sun until he gave up the ghost and died. Amazing as that sounds, I ask you to consider this: All the sermons that have ever been preached in the nearly two thousand years since haven't done him in. That is what astounds me! How is it that the whole Christian movement and the so frequently sorry performance of the church have not finished him long ago? Talk about throwing off your tombstone! How has he escaped the winding sheets of two thousand years of our flawed piety, our twisted theologies, and our blundering worship? How is it the Southern Baptist Convention hasn't discredited him forever? How has he survived our betrayals, yours and mine? How has he survived our stupidity, yours and mine? How has he survived our sad discipleship? If you wish to find the miracle of the resurrection in the real world, work on that. It is Jesus and his way that no one has been able finally to kill.

In the flash of recognition . . .

Resurrection is also encountered in what I like to call the "flash of recognition." Consider Luke's account. Two men are joined by a stranger who falls into step and into conversation with them on a dusty road in the afternoon. He talks with them about references to the coming Messiah in ancient texts. When they arrive at their destination they invite him to spend the night. He joins them at the table and breaks bread. In that utterly characteristic gesture, they recognize the risen Christ. Has anything like that ever happened to you?

Once, in a previous pastorate, after a midnight hospital visit, I was driving on an expressway when I noticed another motorist whose car was stalled on the side of the road. It was past midnight. I kept driving. In my rearview mirror I saw the deacon from our church who was following behind pull over to assist the unfortunate stranger. All unbidden that old story of the good Samaritan came to mind. I knew who was doing what Jesus would do. There was a flash of recognition. "It is the Lord, I said to myself."

I said the same thing when I saw that young Chinese student thin, vulnerable, unarmed, stand up right in front of that threatening tank, its cannon and machine guns and massive steel frame bearing down upon him, and even more threateningly, the eyes of the powers that be trained right on him during the demonstrations in Tiananmen Square. He put himself in harm's way, weakness confronting might in the name of human freedom. In his person I saw another figure in my mind's eye. Was it foolish or unorthodox of me to think to myself, "It is the Lord"?

In hospitality toward a stranger . . .

When Jesus' Emmaus-bound followers reached their destination, they noted night was approaching, and offered the hospitality of their lodging for the night and a meal. They were carrying out an act of goodness, an act of service, sacred to the faith and older than Christianity itself. It is in such actions, Luke deftly reminds us, that we walk in the footsteps of the one who said the person who gives out a cup of cool water to the thirsty in the name of Jesus will not lose his or her reward. The presence and power of the living Lord flashes forth in such a moment wherever it occurs.

Where do you look for resurrection? You look for and find it in common service to those who need you. Mother Theresa said she found Christ in the faces and bodies of the hungry, thirsty, and sick she and her cohorts served. Of course she did. So can you.

In the breaking of bread . . .

When their guest broke bread, gave thanks, and shared it, was the moment the eyes of the two followers of Jesus were opened and they knew who he really was.

Years ago I heard a story about a Christian missionary who was caught up in the hands of the Japanese military during the Second World War. He was in one of those forced marches or death marches we've heard the Japanese imposed on some of their captives. Any prisoner who lagged behind was bludgeoned, bayoneted, or shot. The missionary recalled that he was nearing exhaustion and feared he, too, might not make it to the end of the march. I'm not sure, but I have the impression that night had fallen and it was cold. Just when he felt he could go no farther, one of the guards walked near him and in English whispered, "My mother's house is not far." The column of prisoners trudged on and on, but after a time the same guard walked near again and this time thrust an object into the hands of the missionary. The object turned out to be a hot baked potato. As he handed it to the missionary, the guard said, "Take, eat!" The missionary wondered if the guard was himself a believer, if perhaps he had deliberately used the words of Holy Communion. Perhaps the words were only coincidentally the words of communion.

What we all know is that the stranger at the table in Emmaus did what Jesus had told his disciples to do in remembrance, and they knew him in the breaking of bread. If you seek the risen one, if you are looking for signs of resurrection, or if you wish to plant a few signs of resurrection, you can do no better than to look to the gathering of the faithful and the signature act of breaking of bread in communion. The church is Christ's body, an extension of the resurrection and resurrection power. We become his hands and feet. We are the sign and evidence that God raised crucified Jesus to himself, where he ever lives, ever commands our consciences, and ever inspires our hope of salvation and life eternal.

Vanished from sight . . .

Luke says that immediately after they recognized Jesus, their guest was gone. He leaves us to make of that detail what we will. I can't help remembering when the disciples saw the transfigured Jesus that day on the mountain. They offered to stay there, erect shrines or shelters, and camp out on the experience, but Jesus insisted on moving on. I also remember John's story of Mary, at the garden tomb, trying to embrace the risen one. Remember, he told her, "Do not cling to me so." What are we to make of this? I don't know about you, but it seems to me that encounters with resurrection catch the faithful by surprise, overtake them, as it were, and leave them to reflect upon and act upon what they have experienced.

We see signs and evidence of where he has been, but we never quite capture him. We see the consequences of his presence, but he is somehow already out there beyond us. No sooner have we known him than he is gone. We don't capture him; we never truly encompass the reality. There is always more, we sense, than what we've seen or understood. We certainly can never hitch him like some engine to our purposes. Those who try—and they are many—have already lost the heart of the matter. We can belong to him, but he never becomes our possession in the sense that we own him and can do with him as we will.

With burning hearts in the hearing of Scripture . . .

Most of all, I think Luke wants all who seek the evidences of resurrection to pay attention to the fact that the risen Christ who joined the two on the Emmaus road called their attention to the Scriptures and taught them from holy writ. Later, after they saw who their guest really was, they reflected on how their hearts had burned within them when he explained the Scriptures to them. An encounter with the risen Lord is mediated to the believer through the sacred text by the power of God's Spirit. There is one of your principal keys to meeting with resurrection.

A gift of the Spirit . . .

What Luke does not spell out, but what I must say in closing, is that the flash of recognition enjoyed by the two at Emmaus is a gift of the Spirit. They found the risen one, as did those two, in hearts that burned with the impact of scripture, in a stranger on the way to whom they gave succor, with whom they broke bread. But they only knew what they knew by a gift of insight and on reflection. It was a gift—a gift of the Spirit. So, as you go, look for signs of resurrection. Look especially to the places Luke gives us in his remarkable account of the two who journeyed to Emmaus on the third day.

Michael James Clingenpeel
(Pastor, 2004-present)

Michael James Clingenpeel was born in Ocala, Florida, on September 1, 1950, the second son of Robert D. and Lillian H. Clingenpeel. He grew up in Roanoke, Virginia, and was baptized in 1960 by Charles Watkins, pastor of Grandin Court Baptist Church in Roanoke, and was ordained in 1975 at Grandin Court Baptist Church. While in high school he earned the Eagle Scout award. His father, Robert D Clingenpeel, sold insurance for Nationwide Insurance Company. His mother, Lillian Hatcher Clingenpeel, was a secretary in the Roanoke City School system. Both were active laity. They were early, perhaps charter, members of Rosalind Hills Baptist Church in Roanoke. His mother was baptized at Troutville Baptist Church by George Braxton Taylor, who years before had founded the Sunbeams. She taught children's Sunday school and was active in Woman's Missionary Union. His father served as a deacon and usher, headed the tellers who counted money each Sunday, and was director of an adult Sunday school department.

Clingenpeel graduated *Phi Beta Kappa* with a major in sociology from the University of Richmond, receiving a B.A. degree in 1972. He continued his education at the Southern Baptist Theological Seminary in Louisville, Kentucky, and received the M.Div. in 1975 and Ph.D. in 1979 in the area of church and community. He has done additional doctoral study at the University of Kentucky in Lexington, Kentucky.

Dr. Clingenpeel married Vivian Stephenson, the oldest child of Richard M. and Noralee Stephenson, in the sanctuary of River Road Church on July 22, 1972. Vivian grew up in Falls Church, Virginia, where her father was pastor of Columbia Baptist Church. She graduated *Phi Beta Kappa* from the University of Richmond with a B.A. in 1972, with majors in English and philosophy and honors in philosophy. In 1978 she graduated from the University of Louisville Law School (J.D.) and was admitted to the practice of law in Kentucky, Michigan, and Virginia. She is also on the adjunct faculty at Baptist Theological Seminary at Richmond, teaching "The Church and Law." Dr. and Mrs. Clingenpeel have two sons. Matthew Stephen was deceased in 1979. A second son, Timothy James Clingenpeel, was born in Ann Arbor, Michigan, April 9, 1983. He graduated from Wake Forest University with a B.A. in 2005, with a major in English and a minor in physics. He later graduated from George Mason School of Law with a J.D. in 2010, and was admitted to the practice of law in Virginia.

Dr. Clingenpeel began his career as a youth revival team preacher with the Virginia Baptist General Board in the summer of 1969. In the summers of 1970 and 1971 he was a youth minister at North Roanoke Baptist Church in Roanoke, Virginia. While working on his seminary degree, he was minister to new members at Walnut Street Baptist Church, Louisville, Kentucky (1972-1975). He has served as pastor of the following churches: Bear Creek Baptist Church, Scipio, Indiana (1975-1979); Packard Road Baptist Church, Ann Arbor, Michigan (1979-1983); and Franklin Baptist Church, Franklin, Virginia (1983-1992). From 1992-2004 he was editor and business manager of the *Religious Herald*.

Dr. Clingenpeel enjoys walking, playing golf, reading, and cooking, but notes that he has very few hobbies because the church is his real interest.

Dr. Clingenpeel served as a trustee of the Baptist Sunday School Board, Nashville, Tennessee from 1980-1983. Other areas of leadership include: first vice-president, Baptist General Association of Virginia (1987-1988); chair, President's Task Force on the Denominational Crisis (1987-1988); chair, BGAV Divinity School Study Committee (1987-1988); trustee, *Religious Herald* (1985-1992); and director, Associated Baptist Press (1996-2004). In 1993 he was awarded an honorary Doctor of Divinity degree from the University of Richmond. Dr. Clingenpeel has been involved in teaching since his seminary days when he served as a Garrett Fellow in the Department of Church and Community at the Southern Baptist Theological Seminary 1975-1979, and as a visiting professor in that department in the summer J-terms of 1985 and 1988. He was an adjunct professor of New Testament theology in the seminary studies program in Detroit, Michigan. He has also been a field supervisor for M.Div. and D.Min. programs at Southern Baptist Theological Seminary, Southeastern Baptist Theological Seminary, and Baptist Theological Seminary at Richmond.

Dr. Clingenpeel's publications include more than 500 editorials in the *Religious Herald* and numerous articles in denominational publications, including *The Virginia Baptist Register, The Baptist Program, Church Administration, Deacon, Baptist Standard, Word & Way, Biblical Recorder,* and *Christian Reflection.* He has also contributed numerous chapters in books, including *Shooting the Rapids: Effective Ministry for a Changing World* (Broadman Press), *Choices for Churches in Changing Communities* (Home Mission Board, SBC), *BGAV: The Right Choice* (Virginia Baptist General Board), and *Talk Right* (Baptist Center for Ethics). During his early tenure at River Road, the expansion of the north parking lot was completed and the playground for the children's ministries was renovated. During his ministry, the Preschool Development Center was named national preschool of the year in 2008 by the National Association of Child Care Professionals. He acknowledges, however, that he takes no credit for the Center's great success. He attributes that success to Margaret Collins, the preschool director. He believes that the thrust of his tenure is to lead the church into the twenty-first century as the church transitions from a modern to postmodern world, to prepare the congregation for this transition, and to aid the church in retaining its distinctive identity through this transition. He also considers the call and development of new staff among the most important duties of his tenure.

The Act of Surrender

Mark 1:16-18, 10:17-22

(September 12, 2004)

About two months ago, I sat with the youth of the church on a Saturday, and we talked about church. I asked them what they do during a boring sermon. Never ask a question if you don't want a straight, honest answer. I hoped they would say they had never heard a boring sermon. But I have preached here a couple of times before, and they were honest. You cannot believe the number of answers they gave me. But the number-one answer to what to do during a boring sermon was to wonder if the sounding board above my head would fall. After the pastor search committee and I cleared away other unimportant matters, I asked an engineer . . . and the engineer assured me that it wouldn't. "Probably," he said. "Unlikely," he said. It did not give me greater confidence when the pastor search committee, composed of about twenty percent lawyers, offered me life insurance. But I didn't name the church as the beneficiary.

I want to talk with you this morning about what I believe is the essential act of the Christian life: the act of surrender. Whatever else discipleship involves, it begins and continues by setting everything else aside. To know God, to experience God's power, to live in God's freedom involves setting aside your will and living by the will of God.

Our texts from the Gospel of Mark are the two occasions during the ministry of Jesus on which he said to someone, "Follow me."

I know many of you here are suffering from withdrawal symptoms now that you're not hearing Cecil Sherman, so let me empathize with you. As Cecil would say: Point number one.

When I read these two texts, it struck me that Jesus has chosen to approach ordinary people. The first two make their living off of the sea; they're laborers. They earn their wages with their arms and backs, outdoors instead of at a desk. At night they carry home the odor of their occupation in their clothing. They are the kind of men who eat red meat and chew Red Man, whose idea of a romantic evening is a six-pack and a tractor pull. The other man whom Jesus approaches is a white collar professional. He wears the GQ look, connected, networked, credentialed. He has voice mail, cell phone, pager, laptop, palm pilot. Somewhere along this continuum are people like you and me. You and I are the kind of people Jesus chooses to approach with the invitation to discipleship.

Point number two: Just because the people whom Jesus approaches are ordinary doesn't mean the invitation that Jesus issues is ordinary.

Jesus asks these men to set aside life as they know it and pick up a new life; to say "no" to self and to say "yes" to God; to lay aside the security of the known for the insecurity of the unknown. Whether Jesus goes looking for you or you go looking for Jesus, the invitation is the same: "Follow me," he says. Literally, come along behind me, imitate me, walk in my footsteps, become my apprentice. That's what Jesus asks of you and me.

A few months before my tenth birthday I surrendered my life to Jesus. I did not grow up in a liturgical tradition. Even so, in the Baptist church where I grew up there was a prescribed ritual for giving your life to God. When the preacher concluded his sermon, a hymn was sung, and, if you were inclined to follow Jesus, you walked to the front of the church, shook the preacher's hand and said so. It was that simple. So on a Sunday morning following Vacation Bible School, I moved out of my seat on the second stanza of number 347 in the 1956 Baptist Hymnal, "Wherever He Leads I'll Go." And I reached out and took Charlie Watkins' hand, and I told him I wanted to go wherever Jesus wanted me to go. When the hymn was over, he introduced me to the congregation. A lot of adults walked by, patted me on the shoulder, and said I had just made the most important decision of my life. I was nine years old, and I was a disciple. You and I become disciples the day we take whatever it is we have and are and offer it to God.

In his book *Sacred Thirst*, Craig Barnes describes attending a Christmas party during his days in graduate school. Barnes had noticed that some of the people were exchanging gifts, but one person he noticed particularly for the way in which the gift exchange was taking place. He had the gift in his hand and he was reaching out, his elbows locked, with the gift straight before the person who was to receive it. Barnes came up to his friend and asked him, "What's that all about?" Here's what the man said: "It's not just politeness. I am using two hands so at that moment the person who receives the gift knows I am not hiding anything or holding anything back."[1] The invitation to follow Jesus is to present your life to God as a gift, hiding nothing from God, holding nothing back for yourself.

To the best of my ability, that's what I did on that hot Sunday morning in an un-air conditioned sanctuary forty-four years ago. I could not have grasped the gravity of my decision, but a couple of years later I began to. A missionary came to our church and talked about God calling him to Africa. For the first time in my life it occurred to me that by giving my life to Jesus I might have done an incredibly foolish thing. I realized for the first time that if I meant what I said about responding to God's gift of Jesus to me with the gift of myself to God, then I no longer had any claim upon my life. I could choose, of course, but in the competition between what I wanted for myself and what God wanted for me, God came first. This wonderful gift of discipleship comes packaged with weighty demands. Jesus comes to ordinary people, but Jesus issues a radical invitation.

Point number three: Some people respond to this invitation gladly, willingly, with no struggle at all. Other people have a deep, inner conflict that is set off by the invitation to follow Jesus.

Our scripture lessons give us both responses. Simon Peter and Andrew, the text says, dropped their nets immediately and followed Jesus. If I spent my entire day around fish, I would have dropped my nets too and followed Jesus. It was easy for them. But the rich young man in our other text could not bring himself to divest that which gave him pleasure and security and status. He missed an opportunity.

I find myself, more days than not, struggling when I identify with both Simon Peter and Andrew and the wealthy young man. Like the disciples, the lure of Jesus is attractive to me because in following Jesus, I find myself close enough to the Divine to experience God's presence, nearness, and power. But I also identify with the young man who was savvy enough to understand, at the very outset, the implications of his choice. He saw that when you give your life to Jesus, you no longer have first claim upon yourself. The truth about the Christian life, a life of discipleship, is that some days you know the adventure of it, and other days you weigh the cost and lose your nerve.

A number of you today have kindly noted that you read yesterday in the *Richmond Times-Dispatch* an article about me becoming pastor and having my first Sunday here at River Road Church. If you didn't happen to get the *Richmond Times-Dispatch* yesterday and notice the article, I have a thousand extra copies put in my personal files, and I'll give you one. I've spent the last twelve years more as a reporter than a preacher, so I know what doing those interviews is all about. You look for the good stuff, but in the process you ask lots of questions—and a lot that is said doesn't get reported.

When Alberta Lindsey and I sat down this past Wednesday, we talked a long time for the relatively brief number of quotes that appeared in the paper. One of the questions Alberta asked me—the answer of which does not appear in the paper—was this: "Mike, have you ever wished that you chose another path in your career?" Here's my honest answer: "That depends upon what day it is, and sometimes it depends upon what hour in the day it is." All of you can identify with that. The life of discipleship is never easy, clear, or simple for us.

Point number four: Even so, it is the one life worth living.

Jesus was not wrong when he promised elsewhere to the disciples that they would have life and have it more abundantly. I cannot read these two stories in the Gospels, our lessons for this morning, without comparing the bold, expansive lives of the disciples with the sorrow of the young man who walked the other way.

In the previously unpublished essays of a Quaker named Douglas Steere, published a few years ago under the title *Gleanings*, Steere writes that Jesus promised those who follow him three things. They would be absurdly happy, entirely fearless, and always in trouble.[2] So it was for Peter and Andrew. They lived large lives following Jesus: absurdly happy, entirely fearless, and always in trouble. It's not a bad path. As to the young man, we cannot say. All the text says is that he went away sad.

Dietrich Bonhoeffer wrote about the cost of discipleship, but Dallas Willard in the book, *The Spirit of the Disciplines*, talks about the opposite—the cost of non-discipleship, of failing to follow Christ. "Non-discipleship," writes Willard, "costs you abiding peace, a life penetrated throughout by love, a faith that sees all of life in the light of the goodness of God, a hopefulness that stands firm in discouraging circumstances and ultimately, the power to do what is right in your life."[3]

In 1978 I had the privilege of meeting Norman Vincent Peale, then a fairly old man. That's a story for another day. But it whetted my curiosity when two years later he published his autobiography titled, *The Positive Power of Jesus Christ.* He told in that autobiography about how he came to the pulpit of the Marble Collegiate Church in New York City during the nation's worst financial depression. People were discouraged; progress was slow. One day during his first vacation Peale and his wife Ruth sat on a park bench. She turned to her husband, and this is what she said:

> Norman, you need to surrender your church, your problems, your entire self to Christ. Oh I know you've done this before, but you need to do it again and perhaps even in greater depth. And as you do it. I promise you will receive a peace, a joy, a new energy and a quality of enthusiasm that will never run down.

And then, with all the wisdom of a good wife she added, "And Norman, you're going to sit right here on this bench until you do it." Peale said that he prayed, "I hereby with all of my heart surrender my mind, my soul, my life to you; use me as you will." In the moments that followed, Peale said that he felt a new peace surging through his soul. "I can tell you with complete sincerity," he wrote, "that from that moment on my life has never again been the same. The dear Lord has been my friend all the way. . . . Jesus Christ has the power to change lives."[4] Simon Peter and Andrew would affirm that. For all of its costs, it is a life worth living.

How then do you do it? How do you surrender your life to Jesus?

Another Quaker, Thomas Kelly, in a book, *A Testament of Devotion*, says it's a simple process. First, you just glimpse the wonder of such a life. You glimpse what you can become in Christ. You see the lives of the great women and men of faith and the life of Jesus, and you see in their lives the beauty and power of a life lived wholly unto God. Then, he says, you begin where you are. You start obeying God right now, here in this moment, in this place and in whatever small way you find yourself capable of submitting yourself to God, you do it. You ask God to open your life, to guide your thoughts and to show you God's will. And then, he says, when you falter—and you will falter, all of us who are disciples falter—don't berate yourself. Just start anew and afresh. Surrendering your life to Jesus is an hourly, daily process. And then, ultimately, relax, he says, and let God help you, because you cannot do it by yourself in your own strength. You must rely on God and God's spirit as your helper.[5]

Many years ago Albert Schweitzer wrote a book about *The Quest for the Historical Jesus*, and in it he wrote these words:

> He comes to us as one unknown without a name, as of old by the lakeside, He came to those men who knew Him not. He speaks to us the same word, "Follow thou me," and sets us to tasks that He has to fulfill for our time. He commands, and to those who obey Him, whether they be wise or simple, He will reveal Himself in the toils and conflicts and sufferings that they shall pass through in His fellowship and, as an ineffable mystery, they shall learn in their experience who He is. And so will you, if you heed His call to follow Him.[6]

We do not have sand under our feet, O God, but carpet or stone. We do not have nets in our hands or cloaks on our back. We're dressed in finer things. But you still come to us as you came to those of old and you speak the same words, "Follow me." May we hear you, dear Lord, and may we respond with the gift of our lives, even now. Amen.

Notes

[1] Craig Barnes, *Sacred Trust: Meeting God in the Desert of Our Longings* (Grand Rapids: Zondervan Publishing House, 2001), 128-129.

[2] Douglas Steere, *Gleanings: A Random Harvest* (Nashville: The Upper Room, 1986), 1-2.

[3] Dallas Willard, *The Spirit of Disciplines* (New York: HarperCollins, 1988), 263.

[4] Norman Vincent Peale, *The Positive Power of Jesus Christ* (Pawling, NY: Foundation for Christian Living, 1980), 51-52.

[5] Thomas R. Kelly, *A Testament of Devotion* (New York: Harper & Row, 1941), 58-61.

[6] Albert Schweitzer, *The Quest for the Historical Jesus* (New York: Macmillan Co., 1961), 403.

*Dr. Clingenpeel preached this sermon on his first Sunday as pastor.

The Next Chapter in the Story

Acts 2

(May 20, 2007; May 20, 2011)

This morning I am going to do something I have done only once since becoming your pastor—repeat a sermon. When we gathered as a congregation this past Wednesday evening, I responded to a question about the direction of our church by referring to a sermon I preached on May 20, 2007. In that sermon I enumerated five traits that need to characterize River Road Church in the twenty-first century. This morning I repeat that sermon. Copies are available in the narthex, fellowship hall, and church office.

The Book of Acts is the story of the earliest Christian community—the church. It describes how the church formed and spread across the Mediterranean world. It profiles Peter, Paul, Barnabas, Silas, Lydia, Priscilla, Timothy—the men and women whose leadership guided the church through obstacles and victories. It recounts the momentous events that marked its passage from sect to church—Peter and John before Caiaphas, the martyrdom of Stephen, the conversion of Paul, the setting apart of deacons, the council at Jerusalem, Paul's sermon in Athens, his imprisonment in Caesarea, his shipwreck on Malta.

Luke is the writer of Acts. He also is a participant in the story. At places his pronouns shift from third to first person plural, from "they" to "we."

The heroes in Acts are not Peter or Paul. The heroes in Acts are the Holy Spirit, the gospel, and the church. Acts is the story of the church and the gospel overcoming every obstacle in their path by the power of God's Holy Spirit.

Acts 2 is the story of the church's birthday. Luke paints an idealized picture of the church at its founding. These followers of Jesus are growing in number, devoted to study, exuberant in worship and praise, generous in sharing. This is the church at its best—a vital community of believers full of energy, fueled by dreams.

Exactly seven years ago I stood in this pulpit at the invitation of the pastor search committee. They wanted to see what I looked like in a pulpit robe, and whether I could string together a few sentences that sounded like a sermon.

That day seven years ago I knew something of River Road Church's story, in part because I worshipped in this church forty-three years ago when I was a student at the University of Richmond. Now I know that story far better than I did then.

This morning I want to talk with you about the story of River Road Church, Baptist. In reality there are two stories: past and future, the written story and the yet-to-be-written story, the familiar story and the next chapter in the story.

I begin with the familiar, already-written story of our past.

Congregations, like individuals, have personalities. A congregation's personality is shaped by twin forces: a set of experiences common to the members and a matrix of values that form a genetic code, or DNA. The early events of a church's life, plus its DNA, largely determine what that church will become.

River Road Church, Baptist, has a common set of experiences and personalities that have shaped the life of this congregation: founded by Baptists at the end of World War II, first services met on the campus of the University of Richmond, purchase of a tract of land at the intersection of two major roads in an affluent Richmond suburb, clear vision of buildings that now stand on this property, four unique ministers whose tenures spanned the first fifty-eight years of the church's life, strong laity with names like Hite, Daniel, and Smart who devoted themselves to this dream.

This set of experiences is matched by an equally powerful cluster of values. River Road Church is a church that cooperates with all Christian groups in the community. We provide a home for families split along denominational background. We welcome persons of a variety of Christian faiths without the requirement of rebaptism. We emphasize those themes where Christians agree rather than where Christians disagree. We occupy buildings that reflect the greatness of God. We worship with reverence and beauty. We minister to human need locally and globally. We create an atmosphere of intellectual freedom. This set of experiences and cluster of values compose River Road Church's DNA. It is who we are. If we alter this, we strip our church of its distinct and unique identity; we imperil our future.

In 1965 our third pastor, Dr. Vernon B. Richardson, preached a sermon in which he announced his dream for River Road Church's future. Our church was nineteen years old. It was an eloquent word, and much of that dream has been realized in the forty-six years since it was delivered.

In recent months I have revisited his sermon, a sermon I first read as a student at Richmond College only three years after it was delivered. I have spent no small number of hours pondering Richardson's grand dream.

Has the dream changed? No, but the world has.

Richardson enunciated a dream for a church in the "modern" world. We no longer live in a modern world. Our world is postmodern. The worlds of 1965 and 2007 are radically different.

Peter Drucker, who has written persuasively about organizations and leadership, says:

> Every few hundred years in Western history there occurs a sharp transformation. Within a few short decades, society rearranges itself—its world view; its basic values; its social and political structures; its arts; its key institutions. Fifteen years later, there is a new world, and the people born then cannot even imagine the world in which their grandparents lived and into which their own parents were born. We are currently living through just such transformation.[1]

The issue facing River Road Church is simple: How do we create a church that engages culture in 2011 without doing violence to the core identity, the essential DNA, of this congregation? How do we use our founding story to create a future story? How do we write the next chapter in the story of River Road Church, Baptist?

The answer is not as simple as the question. An answer, however, is crucial, because no one will join River Road Church, profess Jesus as Lord, or be cared for with Christian compassion because of our church's noble past alone. Our influence for God's kingdom depends upon our prayers, worship, witness, and deeds done every day—not upon the long shadow of our history.

I turn now to the yet-to-be-written story, the future of our church. What are the traits that need to characterize River Road Church in the twenty-first century?

The first trait is an authentic Christian faith.

The Christian community in Acts 2 consisted of men and women whose primary qualification was their personal experience with the living Christ. They did not gather for worship and teaching in a magnificent building like the ones we enjoy, possessed no body of doctrine, claimed no Bible but the Hebrew scriptures, and followed no ethical code but the Jewish Law. What energized them was an experience with God that led them to repent, receive forgiveness for their sins, be baptized, and become aware of the enlivening presence of the Holy Spirit in their midst. Their faith was not based on their denominational heritage, a proxy by their parents, or even cultural expectations. Their church had no second-generation believers, no one who followed Jesus because the tide of culture swept them up in its path.

They had a spiritual authenticity in their walk with Christ. It was the real thing. This was no substitute, imitation, phony, or knock-off faith.

People in our culture are not religious, but they are spiritual. They want to know God, not simply to know about God. Their interest is not academic; it is existential. They have no time for going through the motions of religion.

River Road Church needs to be a community in which learning opportunities are experiential as well as intellectual. We do not oppose Christian education, the task of learning about God's nature and ways in the world. Let us, for example, join with a school like Baptist Theological Seminary at Richmond to deepen our theological awareness, and reach out to the students at University of Richmond during the most intellectually formative years of their lives. We are, after all, called to love God with our minds. But our primary task is spiritual formation, the task of teaching disciples to observe all things that Jesus commanded us.

A second trait is a reverent awe before God.

In Acts 2 the community held God in awe (v. 43). Their awe was inspired by the event they saw in their midst. The power of the Divine was all around them. They never questioned that there was a presence and power in their midst who deserved their adoration and praise.

Our culture suffers from a loss of transcendence. So much that what we once held as sacred is now treated as ordinary, common.

We resist this trend when we make worship our central priority. Regular worship is the way we acknowledge that God is the Creator and we are the created; that much of life is routine but God is holy, set apart. So we wear our best, employ music that is not like what we hear at a restaurant or in an elevator, practice rituals that are 2,000 years old, recite words recited by Christians in other generations. This hour is different from all other hours of the week, because this is God's hour, and not our own.

In the twenty-first century our church needs to be a worshipping community where those who enter our doors find worship that is elegant and evangelical, where the Lordship of Christ is proclaimed with beauty and dignity, where the ancient traditions of the church are connected with the demands of daily Christian living, where we listen to God's Word with one ear and God's world with the other. Let us never be embarrassed to feel God's presence as we ponder God's holiness and transcendence.

A third trait is innovation.

When one of our founders, Dr. Oscar Hite, wrote out the distinctives of River Road Church, he said "she dares to innovate and to pioneer." The next chapter in River Road Church's story must include steady innovation.

Though he flunked out of college in the 1950s, Gordon McKenzie parlayed his creativity and dreaming into a successful, thirty-year career with Hallmark Cards. Ten years ago he wrote a unique book about maintaining one's creativity in the midst of a bureaucratic, corporate environment. The title of his volume is *Orbiting the Giant Hairball*. One chapter of his book is named "Orville Wright." The entire chapter consists of eight words: "Orville Wright did not have a pilot's license."

Think about it. Wright did not apply for permission to fly. Nor did he wait on someone to teach him to fly. He was willing to be different, to try something that had never been done before.

This was the spirit of the church in Acts 2. Prior to Simon Peter, no one had preached that Jesus of Nazareth was the Christ; that everyone should repent and be baptized in the name of Jesus; that followers of Jesus should gather in houses, share goods, break bread, or start a movement.

Peter spent the remainder of his life in trouble and died a martyr's death, but Peter never asked permission of human beings because he had the blessing of God's Spirit.

The work of the twenty-first century church is the work of entrepreneurs. We gain our permission from God. We believe there is freedom in the Lord Jesus Christ. We must search continually for fresh opportunities to speak the name of Jesus, to teach discipleship, to connect people to the living God through worship, to build community among believers, to alleviate human suffering, and to pay for all of it with the resources God has entrusted to us.

It is possible and it is necessary to do this without getting caught up in what Loren Mead has called "the tyranny of the now."

Innovation means risk. Will some of what we try fail? I hope so. Let us embrace failure in the service of Christ rather than caution for the sake of the status quo. We must try more than we expect to succeed, remembering that Jesus did not call us to success, but to faithfulness.

The fourth trait is the creation of small communities of care.

The Acts 2 fellowship formed small communities of care. I like Luke's phrase: "They spent much time together. . . ." (v. 46). What did they do when together? Worship. Eat. Pray. Learn. Share. This common life served an important purpose in a world that was no friend to grace and the people who lived it. It was their means of support, encouragement, forgiveness. Moreover, they quickly learned that the truth of the gospel is mediated through relationships more than through doctrine and preaching.

Our age is fractured, busy, distant, individual, rife with boundaries and walls. One of the reasons people seek out church is to be connected with God and with other people. It grieves me when I realize that businesses that sell coffee or entertainment or books are viewed as oases of community rather than churches.

River Road Church, Baptist, is not a megachurch, but we are a large church. Size creates opportunities for us that most other churches do not enjoy.

But size also presents some challenges. One of these is the challenge of community: How do we generate community in a congregation with 2,000 members on roll?

We get smaller. By this I do not mean that we jettison hundreds of members. I mean that we create small groups within the larger congregation, subsets of the whole in which everyone knows your name. We follow God's model. Just as every living thing is made up of many cells, so our congregation consists of smaller units, each one contributing to the makeup of the whole; each one vital, alive, related to the whole.

Hospitality, practiced with intentionality, is a door through which people will walk into the Kingdom of God. Therefore, small communities of care may be our best mechanism for evangelism and nurture.

One of Sir Isaac Newton's laws is that in the absence of external forces, objects will move in a straight line at a constant speed. When you apply a force to an object that causes it to move in a circle, it is called "centripetal" force. The word comes from two Latin words that mean "to seek the center."

Building communities of care within a congregation tends to exert a centripetal force on the congregation. We curve inward upon ourselves, focusing upon us, caring for our own. We can become narrow, exclusive, clubbish, closed.

The force exerted upon the Acts 2 church by God's Spirit had the opposite effect. Instead of being centripetal, the direction of the nascent church was "centrifugal" . . . outward. The gospel was proclaimed in Jerusalem, but soon it spread to Judea, Samaria, and finally to the uttermost parts of the world. They were a church on mission.

The twenty-first century will impart a centripetal force on our church. We will be tempted to provide buildings and activities for our children, our youth, and our adults in order to compete with neighbor churches in the religious marketplace.

River Road Church must resist this impulse to care for us first, and place everyone else second. The needs in our community are enormous. We do not require a passport and plane ticket to see the effects of hunger, poverty, family disintegration, HIV/AIDS, substandard housing, inadequate health care. Nor do we need to go outside our nation's borders to preach the gospel to people who have never heard it in their heart language. The world is coming to us.

Nor can we ignore our larger world. A church with our size and resources must think globally, because the Kingdom of God is not confined to the west end of Richmond. Jesus' Great Commission must never become our great omission.

Every morning a writer faces a terrifying moment. She or he looks down at a blank page. It is empty, unmarked. What will fill it? What if the words will not come? What if they come, but they are weak, lame, ugly?

Against that moment of fear comes a rush of exhilaration. A blank page represents opportunity, potential. The writer's fear is nudged away by hope and faith.

Thomas Jefferson sat before an empty parchment and filled it with the Declaration of Independence. Abraham Lincoln sat before blank paper and filled it with the Gettysburg Address. Martin Luther King, Jr. filled his unmarked paper with "I Have a Dream."

In front of River Road Church, Baptist, this morning, by God's grace, rests an empty page waiting to be filled. It is the next chapter in the story. You and I are its authors.

But we do not write alone. We write together. And we write as those first Christians wrote the story of the church in Acts 2, empowered by the unseen presence of the Spirit of God.

Note

[1] Peter Drucker, "The Next Chapter," from "The Post-Capitalist World," *National Affairs*, No. 109 (Fall 1998): 89.

Living with the End in Sight

Luke 21:15-19

(November 14, 2004)

As you entered the sanctuary this morning, you may have noticed on these outside walls some scaffolding. Don't worry. These thirty-five-year-old walls are sound. This pronouncement has just been made to you by someone whose degree is in theology. The gutters atop the sanctuary building are wearing out and need replacing, and in a few weeks, the scaffolding will be gone. A generation has passed since this building was designed and constructed, and this temple to the glory of God is as magnificent as it was on the day it opened for business.

If you listen carefully to the gospel lesson from Luke 21, you realize this was not the word Jesus gave to his disciples regarding the temple in Jerusalem. It was a Passover week. Jesus was walking with his friends in the courtyard of the temple. They were gazing at the splendor, the wonder, the magnificence of that great structure built to the glory of God; the stones the size of footlockers; the walls rising around them like canyons; the arches and pillars that dwarfed the worshippers. And as they were commenting about its magnificence, Jesus spun around and looked at the disciples squarely in the eye and gestured around him and said, "What you see here all around you, the time will come when not one stone will be left on another. Every one of them will be thrown down. This house," said Jesus, "is destined to fall."

Several years ago I stood in the partially constructed dormitory of a rural camp in a forest outside of Budapest. What had once been used and owned by the Communist party had been purchased and was being refurbished by Hungarian Baptists. It was a robust structure. The floors, ceilings, and walls were more than a foot thick, built of yard after yard of concrete reinforced with steel rebar. "You Americans build for fifty years," said my Hungarian host. "We build for 500 years."

The temple of Solomon was built to last 500 years or longer. It was the enduring heart of Hebrew faith, and Jesus said one day it will be rubble. He uttered the unspeakable. The glorious temple of God would one day lie in ruins. The holiest part of life would be no more. Everything has an end, Jesus is saying. Every story has a final chapter, every play a final scene, every day the closing rays of sunlight, every life the last breaths. All that is precious in life will ultimately fall.

In an article in *Christian Century* in 1995, Paul Duke wrote, "Name any temple you like, any ground that is sacred to us because at one time or another God met us there: a church, denomination, neighborhood, family, friendship, vocation, passion, memory, dream. They all have a lifespan, and they all come to an end."

Jesus delivered that word to the disciples with shocking swiftness. The disciples were never without questions. They asked how, what will accompany these events? They wanted dates, a timetable, an inventory of the events. "Pay attention," said Jesus, "the signs are all around you. False messiahs, false calculations of the time and the place of the end, rulers in international conflicts, natural disasters." Soon the disciples discovered that Jesus was not talking about the end of the temple alone; he was talking about the end of time itself.

All stories have an ending, even the story of creation. The story of human history will come to a close. That is not something you and I like to ponder. I have tried to make a commitment to be a lectionary preacher, to follow the lectionary of the church Sunday by Sunday, choosing the text that the larger church has chosen so I will not ride my favorite pony week to week to week in the pulpit. The day I realized that the text was Luke 21, I began to dread this day. The lesson in the Hebrew Bible was about the great and terrible day of the Lord, and the gospel lesson is about Luke's apocalypse. I'm like most mainline preachers. I want to leave the speculation about the end times to the fire-breathing folks on television and radio, but Jesus is clear. All we hold precious will end, even time itself.

It fascinates me, however, that Jesus did not choose to dwell there. Having said that to his disciples so that they would have no illusions about life and those things in which they place their trust, Jesus got practical with his followers. He spoke to them about the way they should live when the end is in sight, when the present order is crumbling to dust around them.

In 1941, Helmut Thielicke was a professor of theology living in Stuttgart, Germany. He had openly rebelled against the Nazi government in his country. Immediately they retaliated against Thielicke, dismissing him from his teaching position, forbidding him to publish books or articles or to travel or speak to large groups. He appealed. Finally, the government granted him permission to give one lecture each week in the Stuttgart Cathedral Church. For the next three years, as horror upon horror of the Nazi regime continued, as the terror of the allied air raids reduced and pulverized his city to stones, Thielicke lectured one night a week. He did not lecture about the end of the age, though it seemed to him and his fellow citizens that was what was coming. Instead, he lectured about life and about the application of faith to life. "I wanted to show them," he wrote, "that faith not only has something to do with our state after death, but that it also opens our eyes to a wholly new way at looking at life here and now."[1]

Jesus wanted to open the eyes of his disciples to a whole new way of looking at life here and now. He gave several suggestions. In the first place, he suggested that his followers should not be naïve about the future, nor should they engage in idle speculation about the future. There are blind alleys and false messiahs in every age, and it does no good for us to continue in inner speculation about the time, place, or the signs of the end of the age.

Some of you are aware of that series of novels called *Left Behind*. Tim LaHaye and Jerry Jenkins have teamed up to produce a series of twelve novels on the end times. They have sold forty million copies of the novels—400 million dollars in sales, including other peripherals that have become a cottage industry around the *Left Behind* series: screen savers, movies, music, calendars, board games, clothing, etc., etc.

The Bible has only a few passages about the end: a few are from the Hebrew Bible; one chapter from each of the Gospels, Matthew 24, Mark 13, and Luke 21, from which we read today; a few words in one of the epistles of Paul; and then the book of Revelation. Yet here is a series that has attracted the interest of millions of people around the world that is thousands and thousands of pages of fiction. Jesus warned the disciples not to engage in false speculation about the end. That wasn't the way to live in the days when the end is in sight.

Jesus also warned them not to be fearful or to despair. That's not easy. We live in a fearful time. I attended this week the meeting of the Baptist General Association of Virginia in Roanoke. If you were not a messenger to that meeting, you had to carry with you photo identification in order to gain entry into the meeting because of security concerns. It is hard for me to wrap my mind around the idea that a collection of Virginia Baptists represents a target-rich environment! It is the day in which we live, but we do not despair, nor do we remain fearful because the Christian story has an end; an end we already know, and God is at the end of that as sovereign and as Lord.

One of the most interesting debates in theology today is over a matter called open theism. It's a debate over the extent to which God knows what will happen in your life, in my life, and in the events of history—the role God plays in shaping individual events. The traditional Christian position is that God is omniscient. God knows all things in advance: what you and I will do and say and what will happen in the course of history. Open theists argue instead that God may not know every detail of the future in advance. The future is shaped by the decisions of human beings; God has granted free will as a gift to human beings. God is like the master chess player: We make a move, and God makes a move. We make another move, and God makes another move. But the outcome of the game is not in doubt. Ultimately, whichever position you take, we believe in a sovereign God, a God who stands not only before and after and above and beyond the events of this world, but also a God who at the cross became the victor over all the forces of evil in human history. So we do not need to be fearful of the days in which we live.

Finally, Jesus told his disciples to relax and to trust. There would be difficult times, he warned, when you will dragged up in front of rulers to call account for your faith but, he said, do not worry about that. In those moments, you will be given the wisdom to know what to say, so trust. Life as followers of Jesus is a procession of tests. Day by day you have your moral integrity tested, your courage, your patience, your flexibility, your wisdom, and your faithfulness. You will be asked to bear witness to the life of faith, both in the words you speak and in the way you live. Don't worry, said Jesus, trust, because in that moment of testing you will be given what you need—because God provides.

As World War II proceeded, Thielicke continued his lectures. The Nazis would not allow newspapers to announce his lectures in advance, so the newspapers carried a few simple words: Tuesday, 8 p.m., T—short for Thielicke. The people would see that and would go to the Cathedral Church—3,000 people every week—to hear Thielicke lecture on how to live in sight of the end. Stenographers, some 200 in all, would take notes on what he said. They would go back to their homes and copy the notes ten times and send them to soldiers on the front in Russia or North Africa. As the air raids became more and more intense, churches were destroyed, and eventually the Cathedral Church was destroyed along with Thielicke's own home. In one difficult night, after he had ridden his bicycle out of town to speak to a group of people, the air raid sirens came during the middle of his lecture. Quietly and slowly, the people filed out of the church and took their places in bomb shelters while the organist played a hymn. The bombs began falling, the auditorium was destroyed, and the organist along with others were killed. Thielicke wrote:

> What we were doing there was teaching theology in the face of death. There the only thing that was of any help at all was the gospel itself. Everything else simply dissolved into thin air. We were living only upon the substance of our faith and these desperate hours helped us find that substance.[2]

This morning, seven sets of parents brought nine children to dedicate them to God. It's a profound responsibility for these parents and for this church. None of us here can even begin to imagine what these children will encounter in the course of their lifetimes. In all likelihood, one or more of them will live to see the twenty-second century. This we know: They will see some temples fall. They will know some endings, just as you and I will know endings.

Here is what I would like for these children: that they will not spend their days in idle speculation about the future, but when life is tough they will not despair, because they have confidence that the ending is in the hands of God; that God is ultimately victorious and that when the tests come and their witness is challenged, they will be able to bear witness to a living faith that God in Jesus Christ is always present and always able.

Give us wisdom, grace, courage, and faithfulness, O God, to live when the end is in sight. We ask, O God, that amid the many endings of this life, you will grant us the fresh beginning of a faith in Jesus Christ our Savior and our Lord. Amen.

Notes

[1] Helmut Thielicke, *Man in God's World*, ed. and trans. John W. Doberstein (New York: Harper and Row, 1965), 8.

[2] Ibid., 10.

The Glorious Gift of Music

2 Chronicles 5:11-14, Revelation 4:6b-11

(September 21, 2008)

Two words capture the place that music holds in our lives: antiquity and ubiquity. Music is ancient and music is everywhere. In 1997, archaeologists sifting through the remains of the site of a Neanderthal work community in Slovenia found a small flute. It was constructed from the femur bone of a cave bear. The flute, according to archaeologists, was 50,000 years old.

In every age there has been music. Music is everywhere that human beings gather: restaurants, airplanes, graduations, sporting events, elevators, political conventions, shopping centers, weddings, funerals. Music is ubiquitous.

From the first day that a small group of people gathered in the Greek theater on the campus of the University of Richmond in August of 1945, music has been an integral part of the River Road Church, Baptist—particularly its worship. One of the church's first possessions was a portable pump organ carried from place to place to accompany the congregation's singing. Following the employment of the first pastor, the next employees of this church in its earliest days were a quartet of singers who sang in the morning worship service.

When River Road Church had only seventy-five members and an annual budget of only $18,000 the church members gathered together a collection of $10,000 to place an organ in the chapel. And when this grand sanctuary was constructed some four decades ago, care was given so that the acoustics would be right for the performance of music. By intention the founders and the early leaders of this congregation did not abandon classical compositions and hymnody in order to chase the musical trends of the day.

Imagine, if you will, what this hour would be like if we banished music from our worship. There would be no organ voluntary to center us and prepare us for worship, no introit to signal our attention and call us to worship, no hymn to announce the beginnings of our praise, no organ to transition us from the ordinary moment of the announcements to the holy moment of reading Scripture, no *Gloria Patri* whereby together we participate in extolling our triune God, no choral amens to launch our prayers upward to heaven, no anthems to speak to us about the great themes of our faith—creation, redemption, salvation, forgiveness, blessing, thanksgiving—no hymn at the close of the service to invite us to a deeper commitment to Jesus as the Christ, and no postlude to direct our steps out of these doors into service to other people.

I have a lofty view of preaching. What other view can one have with a pulpit like this? Preaching is not a dying practice. Even if the world shuts its ears to the gospel, we can never afford to shut our mouths to the telling of the gospel. Nonetheless, it is a great mistake to consider worship to consist primarily of the proclamation of the written and the living Word from this pulpit. Music is an essential element in our worship, and not just as a warm-up act for the preacher. Music serves every element of our worship. It serves our preparation, our praise, our prayers, our holy listening to the Scripture, our giving of our money and ourselves, and ultimately our leaving forth to serve in the name of Christ. Music is important to this church.

Our first lesson this morning from 2 Chronicles describes the scene from the dedication of Solomon's temple. I wish we could see the temple as it had been constructed in those days. We can only imagine it from its description. It was a building suitable to house the presence of an enormous God. Some 70,000 laborers were involved in its building. There were some 80,000 stone cutters; 3,600 people were used to supervise these. It was covered with gold, silver, bronze, iron, cypress, and linen.

The first act of the dedication of the temple was to bring in the Ark of the Covenant that housed the tablets of the Law. But the second act of the dedication was the entrance of the musicians into the temple—singers, trumpeters, instrumentalists with harps, cymbals, lyres, and other instruments. All of the musicians lifted their song of unison praise to God.

The second lesson read this morning was from John's vision of heaven in the Book of Revelation. Around the throne are these heavenly creatures who are choristers singing, "Holy, holy, holy. You are worthy, O Lord our God."

Here are two vivid pictures. One is of the dedication of the temple of Solomon more than 2,500 years ago; the other is of the kingdom of heaven when time will blend into eternity—what was and what is to come, the past and the future. And the one thing that ties these two texts together is that what was and what is to come, what is past and what is future, is accompanied by sounds and by songs—the glorious gift of music.

So let me give you three words from our text today. The first is that our music is a vessel for a message. When the singers and the trumpeters lifted their song at that temple dedication, their music had lyrics and their lyrics conveyed truth. "For God is good. For God's steadfast love endures forever." That was the song they sang at the dedication. In a world with all of its evil, God is good. That was the message at that dedication.

In a second picture when all those mysterious creatures were gathered around the throne of God in heaven and raising their voices in song, they also conveyed a message: "Holy, holy, holy, the Lord God almighty, who was and is and is to come. Worthy are you our Lord our God to receive glory, honor and power, for you created all things and all things in you were created."

In our world that is ever changing and never allows us to place our weight down on anything, God is in control, God is the ground of our being. In our world that is coarse and ugly, God is holy and beautiful. In our world that regards as precious what is of little value and regards as worthless what is truly precious, God is worthy of our praise. What a wonderful, glorious message is conveyed in music and in song.

When we employ music, we do not do it simply for music's sake. If so, any kind of music would do. We use music as a vessel to cradle and to pour forth the message of the living God, the living Christ, and a living faith.

Our worship team recently has been reading and discussing together a book titled *How Shall We Worship* by Marva Dawn, who is a theologian and a musician at Regent College in Vancouver, British Columbia. She writes, "All our music will help believers learn the language of faith. Music teaches us faith. Music is a prompter in the area of theology."[1]

Occasionally I hear a call for us to abandon hymns in favor of snappy tunes with simple words. We're not going to do that at River Road Church. We're not going to do that because we sing our theology every Sunday. To eliminate hymnody would be to toss out one of the most important tools we have for the transmission of our faith and for affirming the profound truths of the gospel.

When you absent yourself from worship, you cut yourself off from an enormously powerful tool for inspiration in your faith—the hymns. When people keep their children from worship, they rob them of a tool for the shaping of their souls. Why would we give our children iPods and the internet, but keep them from worship on Sunday morning? It doesn't make any sense. Music is the vessel for the conveying of biblical truth.

Second, we employ musical variety. Musical variety is more of a blessing than a curse. When I look at the picture of the dedication of the temple, I notice that they employed singers and instrumentalists and they used numerous kinds of instruments. Variety of music is important, and the rationale for that variety is not so that we can appeal to all of the musical tastes in this congregation. We could not appeal to all of your musical tastes if we sat here for ten hours every Sunday. We have four generations of people in our pews. We have persons who have been Baptists all of their lives and persons who have never been Baptists before coming here. We have persons who are newcomers and persons who are long-termers in our congregation. So we do not employ variety just to appeal to musical taste; we employ variety in music because we have a big God to worship.

Marva Dawn again: "No single type of music can respond to all that God is. No instrument can sing all God's attributes. No era of the church has displayed the fullness of God's glory."[2]

So we will not abandon the classical compositions that have served the faithful and the faith for generations. Neither can we exclude hymns and songs and anthems written by composers in the twentieth and twenty-first centuries. The revelation of God to musicians did not cease when Bach and Handel and Mozart breathed their last breaths. God is alive and well in the hearts and experiences of lyricists and composers today.

This morning's worship is a perfect example of that. Our opening hymn tune was composed in the seventeenth century. Prior to the offering we sang a hymn text written by Fred Pratt Green, who is alive and writing hymns today. We have fifteen of his hymn texts in our hymnal.

He is one of several hymn writers who form what is called the New English Renaissance. They are part of the mainstream of great hymn writing today.

The hymn we'll sing in a few moments at the close of our worship has an ancient text from Psalm 84, but the tune was written by Carl Freeman in 1996 for the fiftieth anniversary celebration of this church's founding. And the anthem during the offering was composed in 1993. So we bring together the old and the familiar anthems and hymns of our faith with elements of that which is new and, until we sing them a few times, will be unfamiliar to us. We do that because we have a big God, and a big God is served best by variety.

Third word: Music, when done well and for the right reasons, invites God's presence. When those singers and instrumentalists presented their unison praise to God in the temple long ago, notice what happened. God's house was immediately filled with a cloud, the priests had to stop what they were doing, and everyone—priests, worshippers, and musicians alike—sat in silent awe, for the glory of God filled the place.

Music has a wonderful capacity to enable you and me to experience the presence and power of God. For most people, that sense of God's presence is less a matter of the intellect than it is of emotion. Words cause us to think about God, but music moves us to feel God. If we are to love the Lord our God with all of our hearts, our minds, and our strength, then we're going to have to employ not only the preaching of the word but also the glorious gift of music that will speak both to our heads and our hearts.

Perhaps you've never noticed it in quite this way, but I noticed it this week. When Mary was visited by the angel and experienced that profound presence, she sang the Magnificat. When the shepherds stood at the manger and saw the babe Christ, they heard a choir of angels singing, "Glory to God in the highest." When Paul and Silas sang hymns at midnight in prison, God visited their cell in great power. When Jesus gathered his disciples and ate a final meal with them, their last act was to sing a hymn together.

Where there is music, there is the presence of Christ; and where there is the presence of Christ, there will be music. Today we gather to rejoice in the living Christ, to worship Christ in praise and honor and adoration. We do so with music, because it is in the exercise of music that we experience the presence of the living one most real and most near.

In this hour, O God, we give you thanks for the glorious gift of music: for ears to hear it, for voices to sing it, for hands and feet to play it, and for hearts to feel it. May we rejoice in this wonderful gift and the servants who bring it to us. Through Christ we pray. Amen.

Notes

[1] Marva Dawn, *How Shall We Worship? Biblical Guidelines for the Worship Wars* (Carol Stream, IL: Tyndale House Publishers, 2003), 5
[2] Ibid., 13.

The Color of Water

Jonah 3:1-5, 10

(January 22, 2006)

The Jewish writer and teacher, Eli Wiesel, once said that "Jonah is the perfect illustration of the antihero, having been a complete failure all of his life and in all his endeavors."[1]

The Hebrew Bible lesson for our lectionary today is from the Book of Jonah. It is about this man who is the perfect antihero. God called Jonah to preach repentance to the people of Nineveh. Jonah resisted. Flatly refused would be a better term.

The Ninevites were the natural adversaries of Israel then, just as their descendants the Iraqis are now. Jonah was pleased, delighted that the Ninevites were to be the recipients of the judgment of God. So Jonah makes an attempt to evade the purposes of God. He books passage on a ship that is headed west on the Mediterranean rather than with a caravan heading east across the desert toward Nineveh. A storm, you recall, strikes the ship, and the crew has a hasty meeting. In order to appease the gods of the sea and storm, they decide to throw Jonah overboard, whereupon Jonah is swallowed, according to Scripture, by a big fish.

This particular detail in this story has prompted an unsolvable debate between the biblical literalists and those who are not biblical literalists: Does a fish have a mouth sufficiently large to swallow a human being whole? Could a human being survive in the belly of a fish for three days and three nights? The nineteenth-century Episcopal clergyman, Philips Brooks, said it posed no problem for him to believe in the accuracy of the story; after all, Jonah was one of the minor prophets.

In the story you recall that the fish coughs up this now stinking and contrite prophet, and Jonah heads for Nineveh, although somewhat halfheartedly. He strolls through the city streets shouting the threat of destruction in forty days. And much to his shock, that very day the entire city of Nineveh repents—thirty-nine days prior to the deadline of God.

Jonah's success upsets him more than had he failed. He could not abide the thought of God showing compassion on one of the Hebrews' bitterest enemies. Frustrated, Jonah goes outside of the city gates and pouts. How could he tolerate a world where both Jew and non-Jew were equally loved by God? A vine grows over his head and eventually dies, and when it dies Jonah mourns the death of the vine, more concerned about the dried-up vine than over the potential loss of 120,000 of God's children, the Ninevites.

Comparing Jonah with some of the prophets who initially said "no" to the call of God but eventually said "yes," Wiesel writes: "Jonah is the first and the only one to reject his mission not only in words but also in deed. He is the perfect illustration of the antihero in Scripture."

What does this curious prophet and story say to us? Is it only a reminder that we cannot hide from God no matter how we try in our life? Is it simply a statement about the deliverance of God for all people? Or is it something more?

Here we have a sharp contrast between human love, on the one hand, and divine love on the other; between human discrimination and divine inclusion.

Let's begin by looking at human love, which often is exclusive and narrow. Jonah declares to those upon the ship that he is a Hebrew; that his faith calls upon him to fear the Lord; that he is taught always to recognize that God is the creator. Unfortunately, though he sees it all as created by God, even people of faith may act selectively or with discrimination towards other people who are different. Jonah certainly did.

Two afternoons every week when I was in elementary school, I rode a city bus from the suburbs downtown to a doctor's office where I received injections for allergies. It was always late afternoon by the time I boarded the bus. I would take the front seats—you know, the ones that are facing each other—so I could position myself to see the driver shifting the gears, moving the pedals. As I sat there, I watched the people who boarded the bus. Most of the riders in those days were domestic workers who had completed their day's employment out in the suburbs and were returning to the city where they lived. As each one climbed the stairs and dropped her token into the fare receptacle, the driver of the bus spoke a phrase I will never forget. "Back of the bus, please," he said. That scene played itself over and over again in front of my eight- or nine-year-old eyes. What I do not forget is that the word he spoke, "please," was never spoken as a request but always as a command. Not once did the driver look the women in the eye when he spoke to them.

Even to a white boy growing up in quiet acceptance of what was a segregated culture, I intuitively understood that it is only in the economy of human prejudice that their bus token did not buy for them the same seat that my bus token bought for me. We would like to believe that that kind of prejudice based on color of skin or gender or social class or economic capacity no longer exists in our society. But even if it did not, what endures is a deep flaw in the human heart that renders human beings as narrow and selective.

Jonah is the patron saint of the prejudiced. He is the antihero. He is the example in Scripture of how not to act toward other people. He could not excuse his calculating indifference toward the Ninevites on being a child or not being able to understand what God expected of him. Like Dr. Seuss' proverbial Grinch, Jonah's heart was several sizes too small—too small to include a group of people who were very different from himself. He reserved his compassion for people of his own kind. He doled out his love reluctantly and then, when the Ninevites repented, he was sorry.

Human love always seems to take into consideration things like color of skin, ethnic background, street address, and dozens of other factors that God never considers very important.

But contrast that—the narrowness of Jonah's attitude—with God's limitless love for the people of Nineveh. Jonah was peevish and sulky. But when you think about it, his theology was not all that off base. When he spoke to God, he said, "Lord, I know that you are a gracious God and merciful and slow to anger and abounding in steadfast love." With his mind, Jonah thought the right things about God. The problem was with the way he acted towards others. Jonah's living did not keep up with the nobility of his theology. He was incensed when the Ninevites repented. Yet God was thrilled because Nineveh was as much God's people as the Hebrews. Let me use contemporary geography here: Iraq is as much God's people as Israel, as the United States is. God is the God of all people and all nations.

Ruth McBride Jordan was the daughter of a Jewish rabbi. She and her family moved to Suffolk, Virginia, when she was only two years old. She described her father as an abusive man, and because of that she left her home in her teens and moved to New York City where she married a black Baptist preacher in Brooklyn. She converted to become a Baptist. Together they founded the New Brown Memorial Baptist Church. She bore twelve children, outlived two husbands, raised a dozen black children as a single white mother in Brooklyn, and every one of them obtained a college education.

One of the children, James McBride, wrote a tribute to his mother titled *The Color of Water*. In it he describes a day on which he and his mother were walking home from church. James asked his mother whether God was black or white. "Oh boy," she said, "God's not black and God's not white. God is a spirit." He persisted. "Well then which does he like better? Does he like black people better or white people better?" "Well, son, he loves all people. He's a spirit." "Mom, what's a spirit?" "Son, a spirit, well, a spirit's a spirit." Obviously James McBride had learned his journalistic lessons well. "Well, Mom, what color is God's spirit?" asked James. "God's spirit doesn't have a color, son," she said. "God is the color of water. Water doesn't have a color."[2]

God is the color of water. God loves all people generously. God is neither black nor white, American or Iraqi or Israeli. God is the color of water. God loves Israelites. God loves Ninevites. God is a spirit.

But God gave us a glimpse into God's character by the sending of a son whom we know as Jesus. So what is God like? God is like Jesus. God is everything Jesus is. Jesus told a parable about a Samaritan who came to the aid of a Jew. Jesus drew water for a woman who was a Samaritan. Jesus forgave a thief who was on the cross. Jesus is love. We see that in the life and ministry of Jesus.

Therefore we know that God is love. God had high expectations for Jonah understanding this and living this. God has high expectations for you and me in the same area, because you and I understand precisely the kind of savior Jesus is—a loving savior.

Barbara Brown Taylor, in her book *Gospel Medicine* writes, "In case you haven't noticed, Christianity is a religion in which the sinners have all of the advantages. They can step on your feet fifty times and you're supposed to keep smiling. They can talk bad about you every time you leave the room and it's your job to excuse them without any thought of getting even. The burden is on you. Because you have been forgiven yourself, God expects you to do unto others as God has done unto you."[3]

While I was working on my doctorate in Louisville, Kentucky, I spent one summer as a teaching assistant for Dr. Thomas Kilgore, then pastor of a church in Los Angeles, California. He was a visiting professor to the seminary teaching in the area of the black church. Dr. Kilgore had been president of the American Baptist Convention, but long before that he was a leader in the civil rights movement. When he was student at Morehouse College in Atlanta, he used to eat lunch every Sunday with Martin Luther King, Sr. and bounce on his knee Martin Luther King, Jr.

I spent many hours with Dr. Kilgore, and one afternoon he told me a remarkable story from his childhood. When he was fifteen years old, he worked as a waiter and a dishwasher in a boarding house in a small North Carolina town where he was raised. One afternoon he borrowed a friend's car, and he and a couple of girls went for a ride. They stopped outside of town, got out of the car, and a moment later the sheriff of the town along with a couple of deputies drove up and accused Kilgore of shouting profanities at a white woman whom they had passed a few moments before. He denied the charge. Nevertheless, he was arrested. Handcuffs were placed on his hands. He was tossed into the police car, driven into town, and booked for assault with abusive language. The sheriff, a man named Woods, tried to extract a confession out of Kilgore, but he was unsuccessful. Kilgore was tried and convicted on the testimony of the sheriff alone and sentenced to six months on a chain gang. Kilgore's lawyer appealed the verdict, saying that his client, fifteen years old, should not serve an adult sentence. The judge listened and said, "If you will leave this county for the next year, then I will not make you serve the sentence on the chain gang." So together, Kilgore and his family moved out of the county into Asheville, North Carolina.

Kilgore told me that in the years following, he felt bitterness toward Sheriff Woods, but decided the only way he could work his way through that bitterness was to pray for Sheriff Woods. He began to pray for him on a daily basis. Years later Kilgore told me he returned to his hometown. As he was driving down the street he looked over and sitting on a crate in front of a store was the sheriff, now old and dying. Kilgore got out of his car, walked over, introduced himself to the sheriff, reminded him of the incident and then said, "I want you to know that I love you and I forgive you."

How could he do that? How could he do that after all of those years? John has the answer: "We love because God first loved us." Our society cannot change the human heart; only God can. And the God who can do that for Thomas Kilgore, and for you and for me, is the color of water. But God is more than the color of water. He is the fountain of living waters, and only when you drink from that inexhaustible supply of God's living grace will you be able to see with God's eyes and love with God's heart.

Thank you, O God, for Jonah, not because he was always good or because he always did what you asked him to, but because from him we learn bitterly the importance of your love, a love that we mirror in the way we treat other people. We pray, O God, that our love would be broad and deep and filled with the kind of compassion demonstrated by the love of our Lord, in whose name we pray. Amen.

Notes

[1] Elie Wiesel, *Five Biblical Portraits* (Notre Dame: Notre Dame University Press, 1981), 137.

[2] James McBride, *The Color of Water: A Black Man's Tribute to His White Mother* (New York: Riverhead Books, 1996), 50-51.

[3] Barbara Brown Taylor, *Gospel Medicine* (Cambridge: Cowley Publications, 1995), 9.

A Speechless God and a Lonely Listener

1 Samuel 3:1-10

(January 15, 2006)

After the Hebrew people had conquered the Promised Land, but before Saul was appointed king of Israel and David slew Goliath and Solomon built a temple in Jerusalem, there lived in Shiloh a boy named Samuel.

Samuel worked in the sanctuary under the supervision of an old priest named Eli. Every morning he opened the doors of the house of God, and every evening he kept lit the lamp of God. Once in the night he heard a voice calling his name. He ran to Eli, but it wasn't Eli's voice. A second time and a third time he heard a voice calling his name and he ran to Eli, but it wasn't the voice of Eli. Finally, Eli counseled Samuel that it was the Lord calling. When the Lord called again, Samuel answered: "Speak, Lord, for your servant hears."

I recall this story vividly from my childhood, and so do many of you. The point of the Sunday school teacher who taught that lesson was always the same: "Girls and boys, you need to learn to listen for the voice of God, because God may be calling you to do something very special. And if God calls you the way that God called Samuel, then be prepared to say 'yes' to God."

At the time, the story of Samuel didn't really surprise me. When I was growing up, all of the favorite Bible characters talked to God and God talked to them. Some voice from somewhere asked them to do daring deeds. A voice told Noah to build an ark. A voice told Abraham to go into an unknown destination. A voice spoke to Moses out of a burning bush. A voice announced to Isaiah, "Who will go for us?" A voice begged Jonah to preach to the Ninevites. A voice asked Paul why it was he was being persecuted. I did not need great training to be able to understand that the pattern in the Bible is that God speaks and people act.

Even so, as a child, while this story did not surprise me, it did cause me to be curious. If God spoke in an audible voice, then what would God's voice sound like? In the 1950s, in Roanoke, Virginia, we Baptists understood that the voice of God sounded like Harry Y. Gamble, the pastor at Calvary Baptist Church. Now, God's voice, I suppose, would be James Earl Jones or perhaps Morgan Freeman.

I also was curious to ask the question: How did Eli know it was God, but Samuel did not know it was God? In time, I learned that Eli knew it was the voice of God because Eli had experience listening. He had heard the voice of God on many occasions before.

In 1983 Vivian and I moved to Franklin, Virginia, where I became pastor of Franklin Baptist Church. Those of you who have moved a few times know that in the process of moving you realize that some of the possessions you own really are junk, so you decide to get rid of them. After a few months, we had a considerable amount of junk that we decided to take to the city landfill. One morning I borrowed a church member's truck, loaded it full of all of the stuff, and together Vivian and I drove to the city landfill. It was a rainy day; the ground was soft. I backed the truck up into the landfill and promptly began to feel the back wheels sinking into the mud. I gunned the motor, spun the tires, and the combination of the truck's load and my ineptitude as a driver caused the back wheels to sink all the way down to the axle of the truck. We became quite stuck.

I looked around and saw another man rummaging through some things in the landfill. He saw our dilemma and began to mosey in our direction. Being a male-type person, I did not want to confess that I had gotten ourselves into that situation unintentionally, so I decided I would say that I wanted to get the wheels real low because it would be easier to unload the truck. In the meantime, I remind you that Vivian was with me, and when the man came up she very eloquently pled my ignorance and ineptitude. So, the three of us began to try to extract the mired vehicle. At one point the man stopped, looked at me hard, and finally asked, "Aren't you the new preacher down at the Baptist church?" "Yes," I replied. "How did you know?" He said, "Well, every week your church broadcasts its service on the radio and I listen to you preach, and I recognized the sound of your voice."

Eventually Samuel would become familiar with the sound of God's voice because he had heard it week after week after week. But that night when he heard it, it was for the first time, so he did not know it was the voice of God. He needed help detecting the difference between God's voice on the one hand and Eli's voice on the other. I suppose God can speak audibly to you or to me. But more often than not I believe that God speaks to us in ways that require us to listen quite carefully to detect the sound of God's voice.

In the book titled *In Search of Guidance*, Dallas Willard writes that whenever we attempt to discern what God wants us to do, we need to keep in mind three important points of reference. The first, Willard says, are circumstances. God's providence is all around us in the form of open doors and closed doors, opportunities and the close of opportunities. We need to discern the circumstances of our lives if we are to know what God wants us to do.

Second, he says, are impressions, inner promptings of the Spirit. The sense that this is something we ought to do or this is something we shouldn't do—the tug or the nudge, quiet inner feeling we cannot explain, the confidence or joy or simple reasonableness of a course of action.

Third, he says, we need to keep in mind passages from the Bible, not so much the individual words or phrases, but the principles enunciated in the Bible. In the absence of God's audible voice these circumstances, inner promptings of the Spirit, principles from Scripture, are the criteria that enable us to understand the divine accent in our lives.[1]

Over time, I came to realize that there is more to Samuel's story than I learned as a child. This is very much an adult story. It is the story of a speechless God in a world that is not listening to the voice of God. It is a world that has become deaf to the sound of God speaking. In I Samuel 3:1, we read that "the word of God was rare in those days and there was no frequent vision." Samuel was born into a world in which his own tribe had become deaf to the sound of God's voice. They no longer listened to what God was saying to them. There was no more manna on the ground when they woke up in the mornings, no more fire to lead them by night or a cloud by day, no more taking a stick and whacking rock and the water would gush forth.

God had become silent in their generation. And we understand why when we see what happens with Eli's sons. We read that they were "worthless men." They had taken the house of God and turned it into a brothel. They had helped themselves to the offerings of the people. And we read in the book of Judges that "there was no king in Israel and every man did what was right in his own eyes." These people demanded their own autonomy from God, and they demanded it so fiercely that God eventually gave them what they requested. It is possible that we can live so long without listening to God that eventually God grants us what we want: our autonomy. When we ignore God long enough, God eventually shuts up.

Some of you have read the writings of the desert fathers. There is an account from one of those, a story about Abba Felix. Some of the brothers come to Abba Felix and beg him, an old man, to speak a word to them. He has been silent for so long. They keep coming and begging and pleading, cajoling, "Please, Abba Felix, speak a word to us." Eventually he speaks, and this is what he says:

> There are no more words nowadays. When the brothers used to consult the old men and when they did what was said to them, God showed them how to speak. But now, since they asked, by not doing that which they hear, God has withdrawn from them the grace of the word. And they do not find anything to say because there are no longer any who carry their words out.

God had withdrawn the grace of the word from Samuel's generation. And God can withdraw the word of grace from you and from me if we quit heeding and listening to God.

But there is in this adult story a message of hope. God's word is rare, but it is not nonexistent. There is a wonderful symbol of hope in this Scripture. In the dark of the night, Eli and Samuel are lying in their respective rooms. But over in the sanctuary of God there is a golden menorah. It was placed there long ago when Moses instructed the people to keep the lamp lit throughout the night and to never let it go out. The Scripture says that "the lamp of God had not yet gone out." And it had not yet gone out because Samuel, the boy in church, was keeping it going.

Never underestimate the influence of one person, however small, however insignificant, who listens for the voice of God and heeds the will of God. One single, solitary, lonely listener can make an enormous difference in this world for good and for God.

Douglas Steere was a great Quaker, teacher, and preacher. He wrote a book titled *Gleanings*, and in it he described something of the events of our nation leading up to the Civil War. He told of a man named Nerius Mendenhall, a Quaker, who took his family to Greensboro, North Carolina, where he became head of the New Garden Friends Boarding School. Mendenhall and his friends were strongly opposed to the institution of slavery. When it became obvious that North Carolina would secede from the Union and join along with the Confederate States in order to retain the institution of slavery, Mendenhall decided he could no longer raise his family in North Carolina. So he decided to move them north and west to either Ohio or Indiana. They gathered their belongings and went to the train station in Greensboro to leave. While they were sitting, waiting on the train, Mendenhall suddenly felt that inner voice telling him to remain at the school. He took it to be the voice of God. He turned to his wife and described to her what he had heard, and she concurred: "Yes, it must be the voice of God."

They took their belongings and put them back on the cart and rolled them back to the school. During the long years of the war, Mendenhall kept that tiny school open, and following the war he took a leading role in the reconstruction of the South. Today, the New Garden Friends Boarding School is Guilford College. One lonely listener—in an era when God was virtually speechless because the people had ceased to listen for the voice of God.[2]

The rest of the story will only take a minute to tell, and many of you know it. The message God gave Samuel to give to Eli was not a happy message. It was a tragic word. Eli and all his household would fall. Samuel was afraid to tell it to Eli, but the Scripture says, "Samuel told Eli everything and hid nothing from him."

And the word of God, which was so rare, turned from a trickle to a torrent. And the Scripture says, "Samuel grew and the Lord was with him and let none of his words fall on the ground." Not one of the words God gave the prophet Samuel to tell was wasted in the heart and mind and mouth of Samuel. And Samuel became the one who anointed Saul, the first king of Israel.

One thousand years later, another boy would hear the voice of God calling in the night. This lonely listener would respond to the voice with these words, "Nevertheless, not my will but your will be done." And God has never let this lonely listener's voice or his words fall. And we would come to know him as our Savior and our Lord.

What a man. What a story. What a God.

We are grateful for those lonely listeners throughout history, O God, who have listened for the unmistakable accent of your voice, and when they heard it, discerned it, and then did what you said. Give us ears in our own generation. Help us to hear, and help us to do. Through Christ we pray. Amen.

Notes

[1] Dallas Willard, *In Search of Guidance: Developing a Conversational Relationship with God* (San Francisco: HarperCollins, 1993), 182-86.

[2] Douglas Steere, *Gleanings: A Random Harvest* (Nashville: The Upper Room, 1986), 30-31.

Contributions

The River Road Church, Baptist, Endowment Fund is pleased to underwrite the publication of *The Pulpit Ministry of the Pastors of River Road Church, Baptist*. This gift was made possible because of the foresight and dedication of church members who believed that practicing Christian stewardship includes establishing and contributing to the endowment fund. The fund directly supports the church and its programs as well as activities that the church would support if it had the funds.

We are blessed to have this fund. As River Road's general needs and the scope of its ministry continue to grow, we hope our support can grow as well. Most of the contributions received by the endowment fund since its inception were planned gifts, primarily bequests. We urge all members of River Road Church, regardless of their age and stage in life, to consider the Endowment Fund in their vision of Christian stewardship. If you have additional questions about the Fund, please contact a Board member or a member of the pastoral staff.

About the Editor

William Powell Tuck and his wife, Emily, are active members of River Road Church, Baptist. Bill has served as a pastor, seminary professor, and intentional interim pastor. He is the author of 23 books including *Modern Shapers of Baptist Thought in America*, *Our Baptist Tradition*, and *A Pastor Preaching: Toward a Theology of the Proclaimed Word*. He was awarded an honorary Doctor of Divinity degree from the University of Richmond, and in 1997 received the "Parish Pastor of the Year" award from the Academy of Parish Clergy. He and Emily are the parents of two children and four grandchildren.

Endorsements

"Are some churches more blessed of God than others, or are they simply lucky in the pastors they get? It says volumes of good things about River Road Church, Baptist, that they have called these five excellent preachers. You are wasting your time in telling me that preachers and preaching do not matter. And William P. Tuck, creative as always, devised in this book a new way to whet the appetite for local church history."

Walter B. Shurden
Minister at Large, Mercer University
Author, *The Baptist Identity: Four Fragile Freedoms*

"To speak of the elevated pulpit of River Road Church, Baptist, is much more than an architectural statement. This marvelous selection of sermons, drawn from each of the church's five pastors, demonstrates the elevated style of scholarly, thoughtful, and faithful preaching that has characterized this church from its inception. Rooted in a deep piety that welcomes doubt and questioning, each of these ministers presents a gospel message that responds to the issues of their day with a courageous faith confronting a variety of social, political, and religious topics. You can read this book as an insightful church history, as a fine collection of sophisticated sermons with unforgettable illustrations, as a fascinating sociological study of a changing church community, or as simply biographical glimpses of five outstanding religious leaders of our day. However you read it, you will benefit from this description of how these masters of the craft of preaching presented the gospel message with honesty, relevance, and challenge."

Tom Graves
President Emeritus,
Baptist Theological Seminary at Richmond

www.ingramcontent.com/pod-product-compliance
Lightning Source LLC
Chambersburg PA
CBHW070739160426
43192CB00009B/1499